SIGNS
of the
WILD

CLIVE WALKER

SIGNS
of the
WILD

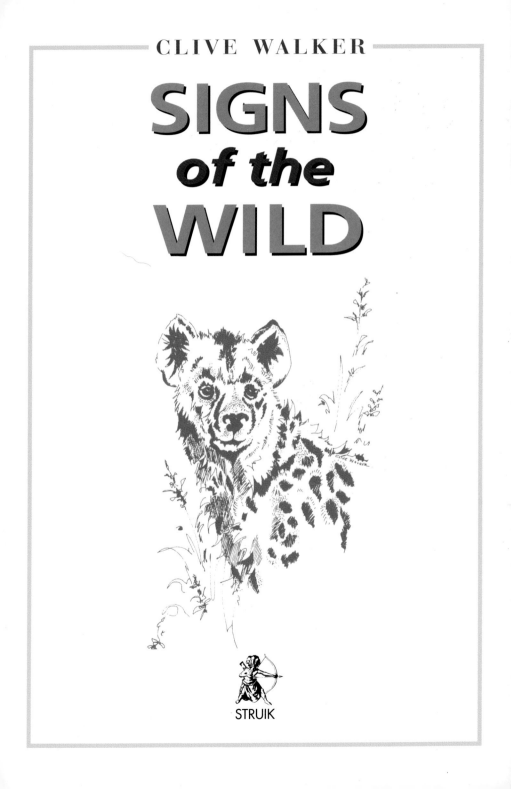

STRUIK

Struik Publishers (Pty) Ltd
(a member of The Struik Publishing Group (Pty) Ltd)
Cornelis Struik House
80 McKenzie Street
Cape Town 8001

Reg. No. 54/00965/07

First published 1981
Second edition 1982
Second impression 1984
Third edition 1985
Second impression 1986
Fourth edition 1988
Second impression 1991
Third impression 1992
Fourth impression 1993
Fifth edition 1996
Second impression 1997

1996 edition:
DESIGN MANAGERS: Janice Evans and Odette Marais
DESIGNER: Bettina Bard
ASSISTANT DESIGNER: Lellyn Creamer
EDITORS: Ilze Bezuidenhout and Jane Maliepaard
MAPS: Lyndall Hamilton
Reproduction by cmyk pre-press, Cape Town
Printed and bound by Tien Wah Press (Pte) Ltd, Singapore

FRONT COVER: *left:* African wild dog; *centre:* Brown hyaena and black-backed jackal tracks; *right:* Serval.
BACK COVER: Black rhinoceros.
SPINE: Giraffe
TITLE PAGE: Spotted hyaena; *page 11:* Black rhinoceros.

ILLUSTRATIONS AND SKULLS: Clive Walker

ISBN 1 86825 896 3

Contents

Preamble 8

Acknowledgments 12

Author's Notes 14

Publishers' Notes 15

Environmental Glossary 16

Erinaceidae
Hedgehog 20

Lorisidae
Lesser Bushbaby 22
Thick-tailed Bushbaby 24

Cercopithecidae
Vervet Monkey 26
Samango Monkey 28
Chacma Baboon 30

Manidae
Pangolin 32

Leporidae
Scrub Hare 34
Cape Hare   36

Sciuridae
Ground Squirrel 38
Tree Squirrel   40

Pedetidae
Springhare 42

Thryonomyidae
Greater Cane-rat 43

Hystricidae
Porcupine 44

Canidae
Wild Dog 46
Cape Fox 48
Bat-eared Fox 50
Black-backed Jackal 52
Side-striped Jackal 54

Mustelidae
Striped Polecat 56
Striped Weasel 57
Honey Badger 58
Spotted-necked Otter 60
Cape Clawless Otter 62

Viverridae
African Civet 64
Large- and Small-spotted Genets . . .66
Suricate 68
Meller's Mongoose 70
Selous' Mongoose 71
Yellow Mongoose 72
Small Grey Mongoose 74
White-tailed Mongoose 75
Water Mongoose 76
Large Grey Mongoose 78
Slender Mongoose 79
Banded Mongoose 80
Dwarf Mongoose 82

Hyaenidae
Aardwolf 84
Spotted Hyaena 86
Brown Hyaena 90

Felidae
Lion 92
Leopard 96

Johannes Phetoo, tracker and guide.

Cheetah 100
Caracal 104
Serval 106
African Wild Cat 108
Small Spotted Cat 110

Orycteropodidae
Aardvark 112

Elephantidae
Elephant 114

Procaviidae
Tree Dassie 122
Rock Dassie 124
Yellow-spotted Rock Dassie 126

Rhinocerotidae
Black Rhinoceros 128
White Rhinoceros 130

Equidae
Burchell's Zebra 132
Mountain Zebra 135

Suidae
Bushpig 136
Warthog 138

Hippopotamidae
Hippopotamus 140

Giraffidae
Giraffe 142

Bovidae
Damara Dik-dik 144
Oribi 146
Suni 148
Grysbok 150
Sharpe's Grysbok 151
Grey Rhebuck 152
Klipspringer 153
Blue Duiker 154

Red Duiker 155
Common Duiker 156
Steenbok 158
Blesbok 160
Bontebok 162
Reedbuck 164
Mountain Reedbuck 166
Springbok 168
Impala 170
Blue Wildebeest 172
Black Wildebeest 174
Tsessebe 176
Gemsbok 178
Red Hartebeest 180
Sable 182
Roan Antelope 184
Puku 186
Waterbuck 188
Red Lechwe 190
Bushbuck 192
Nyala 194
Sitatunga 196
Kudu 198
Eland 200
Buffalo 202

Comparative Spoor Illustrations . .204

Bibliography 211

Photographic Credits 213

Index to Common Names 214

Index to Scientific Names 215

Preamble

Clive Walker examining a blesbok midden.

Years ago as a very young man hunting elephants in the Mahell area, near the Olifants River in Mozambique, I first learnt what wind meant when crawling on all fours – the heavy .416 calibre rifle feeling like some large chunk of lead and not the finely engineered instrument of destruction it was.

We knew they were ahead, because we could hear the tearing of branches and the rumbling, so well known with these giants. I was a complete novice in the art of stalking and well aware of the acute senses of these creatures with which we sought to close, and the wind, which is all important in their struggle with man.

The heat, humidity and closeness of that thick bush was unbelievable and suddenly, silence – not even, it seemed, the song of birds – just nothing. Those who have stalked elephant, will understand exactly what I mean – the silence prolonged and the suspense considerable.

I remember looking at my hunting companion, Hans Bufe, wanting him to make the decision, but he did not have to, for they were gone – on the wind. The wind plays such an important part in the bushveld. Get to know it, and you can make it work for you, but it can just as easily work against you.

A threat display: the foot rocks back and forth.

The best way to study nature in the African bush is on foot, with an experienced guide.

Game trails are being followed more and more by those in pursuit of understanding the signs of the wild and less and less by those in the wake of the gun.

The bushveld is not always the scene of vast numbers of moving animals, but more often empty and silent except, perhaps, for the wind. All around us, however, we find the signs of the passing of many species of wildlife – a honey badger, seldom seen, who passed this way during the night. How do we know if it passed in the night? Do we know its spoor or its faeces? Did we find a portion of honey comb or, possibly, a hole reaching down nearly 60 centimetres with dark, sweet-tasting honey at the bottom? These are some of the questions I have often asked myself.

The hunter-gatherers knew, for it was the source of life. Men such as Selous, Finaughty, Petrus Jacobs and Viljoen knew, for it was part of their profession. Rangers, trackers and scouts know. The black man, in particular, knows for he grew up with it. But what of the new band of scientists, naturalists, trailers and ordinary men, women, boys and girls who seek to understand more of the ways of the wild?

Driving along a dusty track in Sabie-Sand during 1974, we stopped to observe tracks in the fine sand and it was interesting how many of the party ventured different interpretations of what animal had passed. It was here that I determined to study 'signs'. At that time, it seemed that spoor was the most important, but that is only one aspect of many. Later, Professor Bothma of Pretoria University felt there was a need for a study on faeces (dung) and advised me to pursue all and every sign.

Collecting dung is not without its moments of amusement and most people are faintly puzzled when they observe you picking up animal droppings and placing them in little plastic bags.

The project was initiated in July 1974. The study area was Africa south of the Kunene and Zambezi rivers, and incorporated aspects of spoor (footprints) and signs, such as feeding, faeces, markings, and shelters or homes of southern Africa's mammals, the smallest being the tree squirrel. Apart from squirrels, springhares, cane rats and porcupines, the rodentia, chiroptera (bats) and insectivora have been excluded.

Elephant droppings

In certain instances, I have relied on other people's assistance, for although I have travelled through many parts of southern Africa, in some areas I have depended on observations made by others. I must state at the outset that our basic knowledge of much of what we have acquired in our understanding of this subject has been passed on by the black man. He has grown up to understand these things as a matter of course and one can only gain from his experience.

Acknowledgments

It is impossible to write a book of this nature without the assistance of many people. Our knowledge of environmental awareness is a continuing process and in the words of Dave Rushworth: 'If we are to be selfish in our knowledge, we cannot hope to teach conservation.'

The list of acknowledgments is long, from Mozambique in the east to the Namib in the west, the pages of this book are full of their knowledge.

Prof. J. du P. Bothma, Eugène Marais Chair of Wildlife Management, University of Pretoria, for the facilities he placed at my disposal and for checking the script.

Prof. F.C. Eloff, Head, Department of Zoology, University of Pretoria, with whom I had the great pleasure of working in the Kalahari Gemsbok National Park whilst studying the Kalahari lion, and later, in the Kunene Province, Namibia, on elephants. This gave me a rare opportunity to gain first hand information on the desert fauna.

Johannes Naari and **Johannes Phetoue** of Botswana, with whom I have worked and shared many experiences. It was they who, more than any one else I know, taught me the ways of the wild and of elephants. Shamwari from Stabatswane.

The Bushman trackers in the Kalahari – **Tokolosh, Tsipan** and **Houthoop** – the like of their endurance I had never seen before and their observations of desert life were of immense value too.

Tom Moiiamudi, the game guard of Giraffe Game Reserve.

Winnis Watebula from Sabie-Sand Wildtuin – he started out in life as a herdboy with the renowned Harry Kirkman. When Kirkman joined Stevenson-Hamilton in 1924, he tended Stevenson-Hamilton's cattle and then became a game guard under the late Harold Trollope.

The Zulu game guards and, in particular, **Johannes** of the Umfolozi Game Reserve. There are many of us who learnt from these knowledgeable men. **Dhalamini** – the Lake St. Lucia game guard; **Mokabela** – a guide in the Okavango.

The former Transvaal Division of Nature Conservation; the Department of Wildlife and National Parks, Botswana, and the Natal Parks Board.

Jim Feely, Neville Peake, Bob Lawrence, John Varty, Harry Millar, Malcolm Simpson, Michael Brett and, particularly, **Don Richards** – my co-author of *Walk Through the Wilderness* – men who love the bush and who have been most helpful.

Prof. G.K. Theron of the Department of Botany, University of Pretoria.

Prof. John Skinner and his students at the Mammal Research Institute, University of Pretoria. In particular, **San Viljoen** and **Johan Bester**.

Mr. Willie Labuschagne, Johannesburg Zoological Gardens.

Dr. Woody Meltzer and **Eugene Marais; Lloyd Wilmot** of Botswana.

David Rowe-Rowe for information on otters, **Peter Hitchins** for information on the black rhinoceros, **Mark Berry** for work on the bat-eared fox, and **Nicole Duplaix** of the New York Zoological Society.

Charles Norman, Larry Panerson and **Paul Zway**.

The late **Dr Reay Smithers** for spoor and distribution advice.

Val Ford who typed the original manuscript.

To my wife, **Conita**, who has encouraged and assisted me both in the field and at home and, not forgetting my sons, **Renning** and **Anton** both of whom have a great interest in wildlife.

There comes a time in everyone's life when you are fortunate enough to make friends with one of nature's true gentlemen. The late **Hans Bufe**, 'Home from the Hills', is one of them. When I was barely out of school, I faced an African elephant on foot at five metres in the Mozambique bush by the side of this man. A hunter of immense skill, I learnt from him that bushcraft is not picked up in a day. He was a legend in his lifetime and I owe my start in wildlife to him.

1996 Edition

For this edition, I wish to acknowledge the kind assistance of the following people:

Libby Parker, Sandi Eastwood, Koos Bothma, Suzy Ellis and **Ted Reilly** all of Swaziland.

I am indebted to **Jo Collett** for obtaining corrections to the black and white rhino wording in Northern Sotho, Zulu, Tswana, Xhosa, Southern Sotho, Venda, Tsonga and Southern Ndebele. I am also grateful to **Mike Reynolds** for providing additional information on the spoor of bontebok, and **Sharon Montgomery** for photographs, spoor and faeces of the Damara dik-dik.

My very sincere thanks to **Hans Grobler** for permission to reproduce the skull illustrations from *Predators of Southern Africa* (Southern Books), jointly authored by Hans Grobler, Anthony Hall-Martin and myself.

I am indeed grateful to the following who have provided me with excellent additional photographs: Colin Bell, David Lawson, Anthony Hall-Martin, Sharon Montgomery, Phillip Richardson and Professor Koos Bothma, as well as the other photographers credited in the imprint.

I am also indebted to **Ricky Taylor** for the information he provided on the Suni (*Neotragus moschatus*).

To my son, **Anton Walker**, who has spent many hours assisting me with additional information and who provided valuable comment.

I am grateful to **Jim Feeley**, for his comments regarding the description of the word 'white rhino/wijd renoster'.

My grateful thanks to the late **Reay Smithers**, who was not only a great inspiration to myself, but I am certain to every zoology student within southern Africa. His guidance and advice to me during the early years prior to the publication of *Signs of the Wild*, made an enormous difference.

To my publishers, Struik Publishers (Pty) Ltd, especially Eve Gracie (formerly of Struik) Ilze Bezuidenhout, Pippa Parker, Bettina Bard and Jane Maliepaard for their comments, assistance and interest throughout. A publisher's task is not an easy one, especially with authors who live in far-flung places and are only able to be contacted via an antiquated party-line phone. They have my gratitude for all their guidance, comments and interest.

Author's Notes

The spoor illustrations are either taken from field notes and sketches, and from colour and black and white photographs. Unless otherwise indicated, all the spoor illustrations are of the forefeet. I am extremely grateful to the late Dr Reay Smithers for permission to refer to certain spoor – indicated throughout the book by the abbreviation, R. Smithers.

There are bound to be numerous variations due to hard or soft sand, mud and windblown tracks, so one should not regard the spoor as exact. Measurements were recorded wherever I encountered tracks and this, one must realize, will also vary. Faeces will also vary, depending on the season, age and diet of the animal.

I have compiled distribution maps from my own knowledge and various other references. I appreciate that differences of opinion will arise; the maps are intended as a basic guide and, as such, are not conclusive. I have found throughout my search for references that many 'experts' differ considerably and that continuous revision is necessary; basic knowledge of mammals is an ongoing process.

I acknowledge, with appreciation, the assistance of Charles Norman for his most useful references in various species' illustrations.

The taxonomic classification largely follows Swanepoel, Smithers and Rautenbach (1980), with some corrections by the late R. Smithers.

A table of comparative spoor illustrations have been included at the back of the book (see page 204). This should enable users of the book to identify spoor at a glance, by comparing the relative size and shape of the spoor of species that might otherwise have been confused. As a result of ongoing studies, I have been able to make changes to certain spoor illustrations.

Where applicable, Lozi and Yei names have been included; I would like to express my thanks to Mr A. W. Bredell for his help in this regard.

Finally, a number of changes have been made to common names used in previous editions, the purpose being to achieve consistency with those names recommended by the late Dr Reay Smithers in his mammoth work *The Mammals of the Southern African Subregion* (University of Pretoria, 1983).

Clive Walker 1996

14

Publisher's Notes

In this new edition, a number of additions and amendments have been made in order to improve the book. These include updated text, spoor, and skulls and full-colour photographs for each of the species. Nama and Damara names of animals have also been added, where available, to the existing list of African common names and a number of distribution maps have also been updated to correspond with those given by the late Dr Reay Smithers in his work *The Mammals of the Southern African Subregion* (University of Pretoria, 1983).

Scrub hare

Environmental Glossary

Adaptation
The ability of nature, through inherited structural or functional characteristics, to improve the survival rate of animal or plant in a particular habitat.

Arboreal
Adapted for life in trees.

Bacteria
Single-celled microscopic organisms which are found in all habitats, ecosystems or cycles.

Boss
The heavy horn mass at the base of buffalo and wildebeest horns.

A buffalo with boss noticeable.

Browser
An animal that feeds mainly on woody or herbaceous plants.

Carnivore
An animal that lives by eating the flesh of other animals.

Carrion
Dead and decaying flesh of animals.

Commensalism
A relationship between two organisms existing in the same habitat in which one partner is helped and the other is neither helped nor harmed.

Conservation
The wise use of the earth's natural resources that ensures their continuing availability for generations to come.

Diurnal
Active by day.

Drought
An indefinite period of time when little or no rain falls in an area.

Ecology
The study of living things in relation to each other, and their relationship to the non-living environment.

Endemic
An animal that is restricted to a particular region or area.

Environment
The term which describes all external conditions such as soil, water, air and organisms surrounding a living thing.

Erosion
The weathering of the earth's surface by means of natural forces such as wind.

Faeces
Droppings are residues of indigestible food, secretions and bacteria that pass through the alimentary canal to the anus.

Gestation
The period between conception and birth in which offspring are carried in the mother's uterus.

Gregarious
Living in communities.

A chacma baboon family.

Grazer
An animal that feeds on grass, such as a zebra or some antelope.

Habitat
The immediate surroundings of a plant or animal that has everything necessary to life in a particular area.

Typical baboon habitat.

Fruit eaten by vervet monkeys.

Herbivore
An animal that utilizes plants as food.

Home range
The area covered by an animal in the course of its day-to-day activities.

Mammals
The term for that group of animals, which includes humans, bats, cattle and elephants that are all warm-blooded, have milk-producing glands, are partially covered with hair and normally bear their young alive.

Melapo
A flooded grass plain that forms a lagoon.

Mutualism
A relationship between two organisms in which both partners benefit equally from the relationship.

Nocturnal
Active at night.

Overgrazing
Intensive feeding on the vegetation of an area by wild or domestic animals which causes serious and often permanent damage to the area's plant life.

Omnivore
Animals that feed on anything available.

Predator
An animal that lives by capturing other animals for food.

Caracal preying on a rock dassie.

Prey
A living animal that is captured by a predator such as a lion, leopard or cheetah for food.

Pride
A family or group of lions.

Rut
A period of sexual excitement prior to the mating season.

Scavenger
An animal like the vulture or hyaena, that lives by devouring the dead remains of other animals and plants.

Shrub
A woody perennial plant, smaller than a tree, which has more than one stem rising from the ground.

Sounder
The collective name given to pigs.

Species
The term is singular or plural, and relates to a group of plants or animals with common characteristics.

Spoor
From the Dutch word meaning footprint. The track or trail of an animal.

Symbiosis
An association of two organisms in a relationship that may benefit one or both partners. For example in the case of the symbiotic relationship called parasitism, one partner (the parasite) benefits and the other partner (the host) is harmed by the association.

Terrestrial
Living on the land.

Territory
An animal's domain which is defended against members of his own species or other species.

Veld
A local term for open land used for grazing and other needs.

An oribi in the veld.

A tree uprooted by elephants.

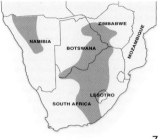

Hedgehog
Atelerix frontalis

Afrikaans: Krimpvarkie **Shona:** Shoni **Ndebele:** Inhloni
Zulu: Nhloni **Siswati:** Nduundvunduwane **Venda:** Tshitoni
Tswana, Sotho: Tlhong **Nama/Damara:** !Noaros

DESCRIPTION

OVERALL LENGTH: 20 cm **MASS:** 0,4 kg **GESTATION:** 35–40 days.
Mainly nocturnal, the hedgehog is found singly, in pairs or in family groups. It has a good sense of smell and hides up in a variety of vegetation, in holes or amongst rocks. This animal is very inactive during the winter months. Amongst other predators, it is preyed upon by nocturnal birds of prey. It curls up if threatened. It issues loud shuffles and grunts when it searches for food.

DIET

Omnivorous; termites, insects, millipedes, centipedes, snails, frogs, lizards, small rodents, young birds, eggs, certain wild fruits and various vegetable matter. It is not dependent on water.

FAECES

Small cylindrical pellets. Food is well masticated, leaving small fragments of exoskeletons in faeces.

Actual size

SPOOR

1,5–2 cm in length; four-clawed toes.

Actual size

R. Smithers

Rare species

Hedgehogs grunt when searching for food.

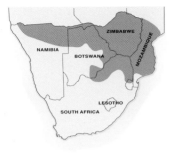

Lesser Bushbaby

Galago moholi

Afrikaans: Nagapie **Shona:** Chinhavira
Ndebele: Impukunyani **Shangaan:** Mhimbi
Tswana: Mogwele **Transvaal Sotho:** Maselale-ntlwë
Venda: Tshimondi **Lozi:** Bunde **Yei:** Unqwa

DESCRIPTION

OVERALL LENGTH: 35–40 cm **MASS:** 0,15 kg **GESTATION:** 4 months; 1–2 young.
As the Afrikaans name implies, these small animals are nocturnal. They occur in pairs or singly and are widely distributed throughout the region. Their eyes shine brightly when caught in a beam of light. Arboreal, they are excellent jumpers and seldom venture onto the ground. They make nests of grass and leaves in the hollows or holes of trees. They are very vocal; the voice is a shrill plaintive cry, but a low, growling noise is uttered when angered. They are preyed upon by a wide range of predators including nocturnal birds of prey.

DIET

Mainly insects, but also includes flowers, fruits and *acacia* gum. Will lap at water.

FAECES

Well masticated; contains fragments of insect exoskeletons.

SPOOR
---

3 cm long; 5 digits with well-rounded finger tips. Slender.

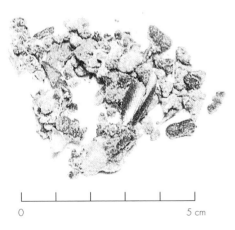

Actual size

0   5 cm

The lesser bushbaby seldom ventures onto the ground.

Thick-tailed Bushbaby

Otolemur crassicaudatus

Afrikaans: Bosnagaap   **Shona:** Chimhavira
Ndebele: Impukunyoni   **Zulu:** Sinkwe   **Shangaan:** Xidweta

DESCRIPTION

OVERALL LENGTH: 60–80 cm   **MASS:** 1,1 kg   **GESTATION:** 123–136 days; 2 young.
Much larger than the lesser bushbaby, the thick-tailed bushbaby appears to prefer higher rainfall areas, frequenting well-wooded plantations, forests, acacia woodland and riverine forests. Its raucous screams can be somewhat alarming to anyone unused to them. These shrill cries probably serve as indicators of territory. It is an arboreal creature but will occassionally descend to the ground. It is also nocturnal and solitary, moves silently and is capable of fantastic leaps. It is preyed upon by large, nocturnal birds of prey, arboreal predators, and large predators when they descend to the ground. When light is shone in its direction, its eyes shine with a reddish glow. Like the lesser bushbaby, it urinates on its feet and hands, thereby marking its territory.

DIET

Fruit tree gum, flowers, lizards, eggs and birds; insects make up about five per cent of their diet. They are not dependent on water.

FAECES

More solid than the lesser bushbaby.

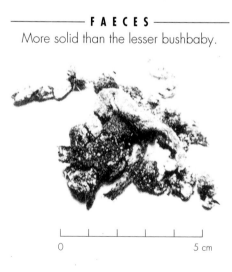

```
0                    5 cm
```

SPOOR

5 digits on both hind and forefeet. All digits have nails except the second toe of the hind foot, which has a claw used for grooming.

Actual size
R.Smithers

24

The thick-tailed bushbaby is an arboreal creature.

Vervet Monkey

Cercopithecus aethiops

Afrikaans: Blou-aap   **Shona:** Tsoko/Shoko
Ndebele: Inkawu   **Zulu:** Nkawu   **Venda:** Thobo
Tswana: Kgabo, Kgatla   **Siswati:** Ngobiyane
Sotho: Kgabo   **Lozi:** Njoko   **Yei:** Unshoko

DESCRIPTION

OVERALL LENGTH: 1–1,3 m   **MASS:** Male 7 kg, female 5 kg
GESTATION: About 165 days; single young; breed throughout the year.
These common, gregarious animals live in family troops or small parties. Diurnal, they sleep at night in trees. They are found in a wide range of habitats, including tree and bush savanna, montane and riverine forest and coastal bush. Not strictly arboreal, they take readily to the ground in search of food and water. Their senses are acute and they are constantly on the alert against predators such as leopard and the crowned eagle (*Stephanoaetus coronatus*). The call most often heard is a chatter and stutter, or a high pitched squeal when in distress. They are often kept as pets when young, which should be avoided as they can become treacherous when older. The social order is always maintained, often aggressively.

DIET

Omnivorous, although principally vegetarian; also eat nesting birds, birds' eggs, lizards, insects and scorpions – in fact virtually anything edible. Fond of crops. Not dependent on water when fruit is available.

SPOOR

Hind feet approximately 7 cm long.

Hind foot
7,5–9 cm

Forefoot
6 cm

The vervet monkey is not strictly arboreal.

FAECES

Often contain seeds of fruit. Grass and vegetable matter are also evident in the droppings.

0   5 cm

Samango Monkey

Cercopithecus mitis

Afrikaans: Samango-aap **Shona:** Dongonda
Ndebele: Insimango **Xhosa, Zulu, Siswati:** Nsimango
Shangaan: Ndlandlama **Venda:** Dulu

DESCRIPTION

OVERALL LENGTH: Up to 1,4 m **MASS:** Male up to 9 kg; female up to 7 kg
GESTATION: 140 days; single young born during the summer months.

Not as common as the vervet monkey due to its very restricted range, the samango monkey is principally arboreal and diurnal, resting at night in trees in small groups. Solitary males are often encountered, otherwise they are found in troops or family groups. Found in the eastern regions of southern Africa in forested areas, the range includes the Zimbabwean Eastern Highlands and extends into Mpumalanga, usually in high rainfall areas. It is heavier than the vervet monkey and not as prone to crop raiding. It is preyed upon by the crowned eagle (*Stephanoaetus coronatus*) and leopard. This highly vocal species emits many sounds, from a distinctive deep boom to the most frequently issued sound, a high-pitched, repeated 'nyah'.

DIET

Omnivorous; gum, flowers, fruits, vegetable matter, insects and birds' eggs.

SPOOR

Larger than that of the vervet monkey, though smaller than the chacma baboon.

FAECES

Larger than the vervet monkey, although similar in content.

0   5 cm

Rare species

Actual size

The samango monkey rests in a tree at night.

Chacma Baboon

Papio ursinus

Afrikaans: Bobbejaan **Shona:** Bveni, Gudo
Ndebele: Indwanguly **Siswati:** Mfene
Tswana/Sotho: Tshwene **Venda:** Pfene **Lozi:** Pombwe
Yei: Uwurutwa **Nama/Damara:** | Norab, | Nerab, || Erub

DESCRIPTION

SHOULDER HEIGHT: 80 cm **MASS:** Male 30 kg, female 18 kg
GESTATION: 6–7 months; single young.

These large, powerfully built primates have a prominent, dog-like muzzle, and a strong jaw with canines which exceed those of a lion in length. They are terrestrial, gregarious animals and are found in small and large troops. They possess considerable intelligence and have acute eyesight and hearing. Their enemies are leopard and man. They will often be found in the company of antelope, whose additional alertness supplements their own. They frequent several sleeping sites, occupying a large tree or ledges on mountain slopes. Noisy at dawn and dusk, they issue loud, deep barks with a range of conversational utterings, shrieks and screams. Baboons have a well-developed social structure and when danger threatens, the dominant males adopt a hostile stance to protect the agile and swift troop, which rapidly disperses. The flanking members stand up in the grass or jump on to anthills or tree trunks to keep the threat in view. On occasions, when I have been on foot and disturbed baboons, my sudden presence has caused them to disappear in a free-for-all – every baboon for himself. They are fearful of leopard and will jump considerable distances in an effort to escape, all the while uttering the wildest cries.

DIET

Omnivorous; fruits, leaves, tubers, roots, bulbs, scorpions (they are most adept at removing the sting from the tail), ground birds, eggs, insects and young mammals. Partial to crop raiding and will, in fact, eat virtually anything. Dependent on water.

FAECES

Baboons have no set pattern and their dung is found over a wide area as they move and feed. The ground under roosting spots is usually scattered with dung.

Chacma baboons are found in small or large groups.

Note the largeness of the hind foot. The forefoot clearly shows the knuckles.

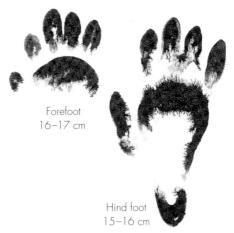

Forefoot
16–17 cm

Hind foot
15–16 cm

Pangolin

Manis temminckii

Other names in English: Scaly anteater, Temminck's pangolin.
Afrikaans: letermagog **Shona:** Haka, Hambakubvu
Ndebele: Inkakha **Siswati:** Finyeti **Sotho/Tswana:**
Kgaga **Venda:** Khwara **Shangaan:** Shikwaru
Lozi: Nake **Yei:** Unkaka **Nama/Damara:** ‖ Khommi

―――――――――― **D E S C R I P T I O N** ――――――――――

OVERALL LENGTH: Up to 1 m **MASS:** Up to 8 kg **GESTATION:** 150 days; single young.
This is a rare, mainly nocturnal animal that lives in holes (dug either by itself or by other animals such as the aardvark) or under dense bush. When placed under stress, it curls up tightly in a ball with its head and feet firmly tucked in. It moves along on its hind legs, occasionally dropping onto all fours or using the tail and forelegs for balance. It is highly regarded by many Africans due to their superstitious beliefs and for its medicinal properties – which may account for its rarity. Products are often found in *muti* (traditional medicine) shops. It has extremely good hearing.

―――――――――――――――― **D I E T** ――――――――――――――――

Eats certain species of termites and ants. It does not possess teeth, but has a well-developed muscular stomach which is used to grind up ants and termites, with the help of ingested gravel.

―――――――――――――――― **S P O O R** ――――――――――――――――

The claws are prominent. Claws 2, 3 and 4 are well-developed and recurved (bent backwards). Walks mainly on its hind legs in an upright position.

Forefoot
5 cm

Hind foot
Actual size

Endangered species

32

The pangolin's distinctive scales cover the upperparts, sides and tail.

The smudge-like impression of the hind foot.

FAECES

Consist mainly of exoskeletons of ants and termites, as well as the sand that is ingested while feeding; similar to the aardvark (see page 112).

Scrub Hare
Lepus saxatilis

Afrikaans: Kolhaas **Shona:** Tsuro **Ndebele:** Umvundla
Zulu: Logwaja **Shangaan:** Mpfundla **Tswana:** Mmutlwa
Venda: Muvhuda, Khomu **Southern Sotho:** Mofuli
Siswati: Logwatja **Lozi:** Shakame **Yei:** Unshuru
Nama/Damara: !Ôas

DESCRIPTION

OVERALL LENGTH: 40–65 cm **MASS:** Up to 2 kg **GESTATION:** 30 days.
This usually silent animal is found singly or, occasionally, in pairs. Mainly nocturnal, it is widely distributed throughout southern Africa. It occurs in woodland and grassy scrub cover. Preyed upon by owls, pythons and carnivores, including cheetah which run them down, it lies up in thick grass and under bushes with the ears held flat against the head. When in danger, it darts off at the last moment with a swift, jinking run. More robust in build than the Cape hare, it has no flank stripe.

DIET
Predominantly grazes, but will feed on other plants. Not dependent on water.

SPOOR
Forefoot is 2 cm long; the hind foot is 3 cm long.

FAECES
Well-rounded pellets about 1 cm in diameter. Similar in all species.

Forefoot
Actual size

Hind foot
Actual size

0   5 cm

The scrub hare is widely distributed throughout southern Africa.

Cape Hare
Lepus capensis

Afrikaans: Vlakhaas **Shona:** Tsuro **Ndebele:** Umvundla
Zulu: Logwaja **Shangaan:** Mpfundla **Tswana:** Mmutlwa
Venda: Muvhuda, Khomu **Southern Sotho:** Mofuli
Siswati: Logwatja **Lozi:** Shakame **Yei:** Unshuru
Nama/Damara: !Ôas

DESCRIPTION

OVERALL LENGTH: 45–60 cm **MASS:** up to 2,5 kg **GESTATION:** 30 days.
The Cape hare has a wide distribution in the western and central areas of southern
Africa. Slightly lighter in mass and more fragile-looking than the scrub hare, the
Cape is found in drier, more open habitat. Mainly nocturnal, it has a clearly
defined buffy flank stripe, which is less obvious in arid areas.

DIET

Vegetarian. Not dependent on water.

FAECES

Well-rounded pellets, about 1 cm in
diameter. Same as the scrub hare.

SPOOR

Forefoot is 2 cm long; hind foot is
3 cm long.

Forefoot
Actual size

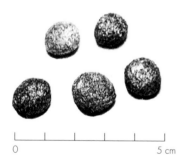

0   5 cm

Hind foot
Actual size

The Cape hare is found in dry, open habitat.

Ground Squirrel

Xerus inauris

Afrikaans: Waaierstertgrondeekhoring
Tswana: Sekatamosima

DESCRIPTION

OVERALL LENGTH: About 45 cm long   **MASS:** Up to 1 kg   **GESTATION:** 40–50 days; 1–3 young born throughout the year, peaking in May and August.

Ground squirrels are purely terrestrial and live in arid, open terrain with sparse bush cover. They are found in the Northern Cape, southwestern Botswana and Namibia. Highly sociable, they live in large groups in burrows up to 183 metres in length, which they excavate themselves. Colonies are dominated by females.

Strictly diurnal, they are wary of predators, although casual about concealing themselves. They enjoy basking in the sun and taking 'sand baths' and, when alarmed, issue a high-pitched whistle. Adults growl during aggressive encounters and the young chirp. They are preyed upon by eagles and most of the wild cats.

DIET

Predominantly vegetarian; roots, tubers, bulbs, stems of grass and seeds. Also eat insects. Appears to be independent of water.

FAECES

Droppings are similar to the scrub hare but longer. Average size is 1,5 cm long and 0,5 cm wide.

SPOOR

Not collected.

0   5 cm

The ground squirrel uses its bushy tail to shield it from the sun.

Tree Squirrel
Paraxerus cepapi

Afrikaans: Boomeekhoring **Shona:** Tsindi
Ndebele: Ubusinti **Venda:** Tshithura **Shangaan:** Sindyane
Tswana: Setlhora/Sepêpê **Lozi:** Kamale **Yei:** Unshindi
Nama/Damara: Haritatōb

DESCRIPTION

OVERALL LENGTH: 35 cm **MASS:** 0,2 kg **GESTATION:** About 55 days.

The tree squirrel is solitary or found in pairs. It is diurnal and arboreal, although it spends a large percentage of its time on the ground in search of food. If it is disturbed it makes great haste in retreating to the nearest tree. It lives in holes in trees, lining the nest with grasses. Distribution extends from northern Zululand, Mozambique, Mpumalanga, Rustenburg and Waterberg areas, through to southeastern Botswana and Zimbabwe. Very vocal, its peculiar call is often mistaken for that of a bird. It is preyed upon by the black mamba, hawks, genets, wild cats, pythons and mongooses.

DIET

Vegetarian; a wide variety of plant food including leaves, wild fruits and roots.

SPOOR

Detail of spoor supplied by the late R. Smithers.

FAECES

Mouse-like in appearance.

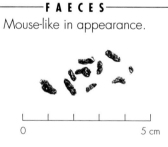

```
0                    5 cm
```

Forefoot

Hind foot

Actual size

Tree squirrels live in holes in trees.

Springhare
Pedetes capensis

Afrikaans: Springhaas **Ndebele:** Umahelane
Shona: Nhire, Gwidzu **Zulu:** Ndlulane
Shangaan: Xindjengwe **Southern Sotho:** Tshipjane
Tswana: Tshipô **Venda:** Khadzimutavha **Siswati:** Ndlulwane
Lozi: Sinkuyu **Yei:** Unkuyu **Nama/Damara:** ǂGōb

--------------------------------- D E S C R I P T I O N ---------------------------------

OVERALL LENGTH: 70–85 cm **MASS:** 3 kg **GESTATION:** 45 days.
Purely nocturnal, the spring hare's eyes shine brightly in a spotlight. It lives in pairs, often in large communities in burrows excavated in sandy soils. With its long and powerful hindlegs and short, lightly built forelegs, it is swift and kangaroo-like. This creature has acute senses. The flesh is much sought after by certain tribes and in Botswana it forms a part of the bushman's diet.

--------------------------------- D I E T ---------------------------------

Vegetarian; mainly the stems of grasses, bulbs, roots, and cultivated crops.

----------- F A E C E S -----------
2 cm long.

----------- S P O O R -----------
Hind foot has a three-toed impression. Forefoot has 5 long, pointed claws used for digging.

0   5 cm

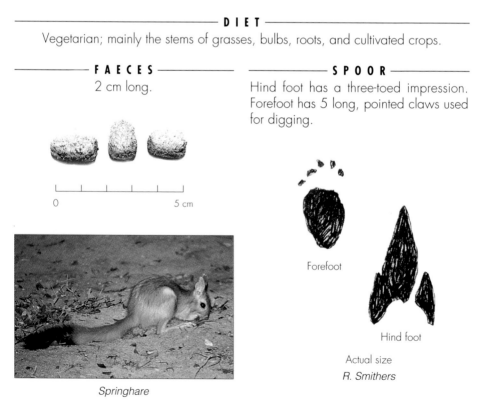

Forefoot

Hind foot

Actual size
R. Smithers

Springhare

Greater Cane-rat

Thryonomys swinderianus

Afrikaans: Grootrietrot **Shona:** Tsenzi **Ndebele:** Ivondo
Zulu, Siswati: Vondo **Shangaan:** Nhleti **Tswana:** Bodi
Venda: Tshedzi **Transvaal Sotho:** Tswidi **Lozi:** Siumbi
Yei: Unsenze

DESCRIPTION

OVERALL LENGTH: 60–80 cm **MASS:** 4–5 kg **GESTATION:** 90 days; up to 4 young.
Widespread throughout eastern southern Africa, the greater cane-rat is nocturnal. Gregarious but often found singly, it swims exceptionally well and will take to water readily. Its presence in an area is noticeable by the 'runs' it creates through grass and general vegetation. Mainly found on the edges of swamps, vleis, river banks, dams and sugar cane plantations. The young are born in burrows lined with grasses. The greater cane-rat is preyed upon by a large range of carnivores, and especially eagles and pythons. The meat is highly prized by Zulus as a food source.

DIET

Reeds, aquatic grasses, other types of grasses, fruits, bark and crops. They are well known for crop raiding, particularly sugar cane.

FAECES

Similar to the spring hare; 2,5 cm long.

SPOOR

Has not been observed in the wild.

0   5 cm

Greater cane-rat

Porcupine
Hystrix africaeaustralis

Afrikaans: Ystervark **Zulu:** Nungu **Siswati:** Ngungubane
Shangaan: Nungu **Tswana, Transvaal Sotho:** Noko
Venda: Nungu **Lozi:** Sinuku **Yei:** Unungu
Nama/Damara: !Noab

DESCRIPTION

OVERALL LENGTH: 80 cm **MASS:** Up to 18 kg **GESTATION:** 93–94 days.
The porcupine is the largest African rodent. It tolerates and has successfully adapted to a wide range of habitats and is distributed throughout southern Africa. It frequents disused antbear holes, holes which it has dug itself, caves or rocky crevices. Here it raises its young or lies up. Found alone, in pairs or in small groups, it is nocturnal.
It is armed with lethal quills which it rattles when annoyed or alarmed. If this fails it will attack in a sideways and backwards running action, in an attempt to impale the attacker. It does not shoot its quills. Principal enemies are lion and leopard, although they attack at their own peril.

DIET

Vegetarian. Capable of doing great damage to crops. It is fond of tree bark and will also gnaw bones and ivory, which accounts for the absence of these when a dead elephant is found in a remote area.

FAECES

Easily recognizable, being shaped like a series of fibrous, elongated fire crackers often attached to one another.

```
L__I__I__I__I__I
0              5 cm
```

The porcupine is armed with lethal quills which it rattles when alarmed or annoyed.

Hind foot elongated, up to 9 cm long; forefoot 5–6 cm long.

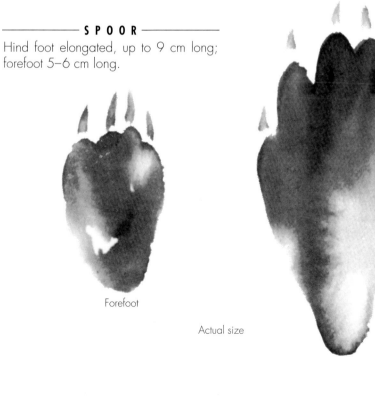

Forefoot

Actual size

Hind foot

Wild Dog
Lycaon pictus

Afrikaans: Wildehond **Shona:** Mhumhi **Ndebele:** Inganyana
Shangaan: Hlolwa **Tswana:** Letlhalerwa **Venda:** Dalerwa
Zulu: Nkontshane **Sotho:** Tlalerwa **Siswati:** Budzatje
Lozi: Liakanyani **Yei:** Umenzi **Nama/Damara:** !Gaub

DESCRIPTION

SHOULDER HEIGHT: 65 cm **MASS:** 24–30 kg **GESTATION:** 69–70 days.

Killers in carnival suits, wild dogs have a poor reputation and have been reduced to very low numbers in southern Africa – although they probably occur in reasonable numbers in Botswana. Game farms have also eliminated them which is most short-sighted as they move around continuously, occupying large home ranges. They are fearless and have considerable stamina which is required for running down their prey. Wild dogs can reach a top speed of 64 km per hour and can maintain a speed of about 45 km per hour for nearly 5 km. They kill about 85 per cent of the prey they pursue. They have a well-ordered social structure and may be found in packs of up to 30 or 40 individuals. The inquisitive nature of wild dogs may cause alarm, but no case exists where humans have come to harm. They produce a soft clicking sound and have a deep, hoarse bark. Their eyesight is good. Various breeding programmes are on the go in an effort to re-introduce them at De Wildt, under the supervision of Anne van Dyk, and at Hoedspruit.

DIET

Prey on a wide range of animals, from small to large mammals, and domestic stock. Will also consume the prey of other predators. Parents regurgitate food for the litter. Drink regularly but can go for long periods without water.

FAECES

Dog-like, elongated, often full of hair.

0   5 cm

0   20 cm

Endangered species

The wild dog is easily identified by the unusual blotched pattern of its coat.

SPOOR

7,5 cm long; neat, elongated track with distinctive claw marks.

Actual size

Cape Fox
Vulpes chama

Afrikaans: Silwervos
Southern Sotho: Mophèmè   **Tswana:** Lesie
Nama/Damara: !Khamab

DESCRIPTION

SHOULDER HEIGHT: 30–33 cm   **MASS:** 3,6–4,5 kg
GESTATION: About 56 days; 3–5 young in a litter.

The only true fox to be found in southern Africa, this species inhabits dry, open veld and Kalahari savanna. Distribution ranges from the Northern Cape and the Free State, to southern Botswana and Namibia. The Cape fox is mainly nocturnal and is found singly or in pairs. It lives and raises its young in burrows, but will also lie up under dense scrub. The voice is not unlike that of the European fox.

DIET
Small mammals, insects, birds, eggs of ground birds.

FAECES
Similar to the black-backed jackal.

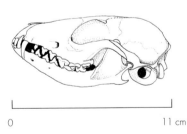

0   11 cm

0   5 cm

The Cape fox is mainly nocturnal in habit.

──────── SPOOR ────────

4,5 cm in length; 5 toes on the forefeet and 4 on the hind feet. Feet are similar to that of the black-backed jackal but slightly narrower.

Actual size

Bat-eared Fox

Otocyon megalotis

Afrikaans: Bakoorvos **Transvaal Sotho:** Motlhose
Tswana: Thlose **Ndebele:** Unga **Shona:** Gava
Nama/Damara: ǁ Āb

D E S C R I P T I O N

OVERALL LENGTH: 86–97 cm **SHOULDER HEIGHT:** 30 cm **MASS:** 2,5–4 kg
GESTATION: 60–70 days.

The bat-eared fox is not, as its name implies, a true fox. The bushy, black-tipped tail, black-edged ears and blackish legs make this animal easily distinguishable. It has the ability to twist and turn whilst running after prey or when escaping a predator, such as one of the large eagles. Both diurnal and nocturnal, it occurs in pairs or small groups and lives in burrows which it digs itself, in old antbear holes or under bushes. It has well-developed senses. The call is not a howl, but a series of soft, shrill 'who-who' sounds. It is found in Botswana, Namibia, the western fringe of Zimbabwe, and in the Northern Cape, southwestern Cape, North-West Province, Northern Province and the Free State in South Africa.

D I E T

Insects, small rodents, fruits, ground-nesting birds, small reptiles and larvae. The large, well-developed ears enable it to detect underground prey which it digs out.

S P O O R

A neat, narrow foot.

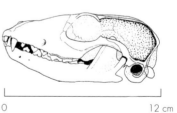

0   12 cm

F A E C E S

Round and compact; often containing fragments of exoskeletons.
(Collected by M. Berry)

Actual size

This species has distinctive black-edged ears.

Midden area

0   5 cm

Black-backed Jackal

Canis mesomelas

Afrikaans: Rooijakkals **Zulu:** Mpungutshe, Khanka
Siswati: Mpungutje **Shangaan:** Impungutshe **Ndebele:** Ikhanka
Shona: Hungubwe **Tswana:** Phokojwe **Venda:** Phungubwe
Sotho: Phokobje, Phokojoe **Nama/Damara:** ǀGirib, ǀgireb

--- **DESCRIPTION** ---

SHOULDER HEIGHT: 40 cm **MASS:** up to 13 kg **GESTATION:** 60 days; up to 6 pups.
The black-backed jackal is a handsome species that occurs throughout southern Africa. The distinctive cry is well known and it communicates with an elaborate vocabulary. Mainly nocturnal, it is found singly or in pairs. Large numbers will congregate at a carcass. It is cunning and swift and will wait in the wings for lions to finish eating, often darting in to snatch a morsel. During the day it rests up under low bushes. The young are born in abandoned antbear holes. Sight, sense of smell and hearing are acute. It is preyed upon by leopard, which have a preference for canine meat; large eagles will also take young pups.

--- **DIET** ---

Carrion, rodents, reptiles, gamebirds, insects, eggs, fruit and hares. Hunts young antelope and will prey on small, young livestock. Drinks water regularly.

--- **FAECES** ---

Small, dog-like in appearance.

0   5 cm

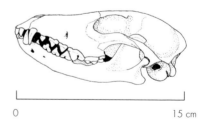

0   15 cm

The black-backed jackal is easily recognized by its distinctive black 'saddle'.

—————— SPOOR ——————
Neat, small, dog-like tracks.

Actual size

Side-striped Jackal

Canis adustus

Afrikaans: Witkwasjakkals Zulu: Mpungutshe Venda: Dabe
Tswana: Rantalàje Shangaan: Hlati Shona: Gava
Ndebele: Ikhanka Siswati: Inkalwane Lozi: Luwawa

DESCRIPTION

SHOULDER HEIGHT: 40 cm **MASS:** 8–12 kg **GESTATION:** 60 days.
Fairly silent animals, except for an owl-like hoot, quite unlike the customary howl of the black-backed jackal. They are found singly or in pairs. The Bayei people of the Okavango Swamps believe their appearance signals the presence of lion. They are lighter in mass and do not have the distinctive saddle of the black-backed jackal. The tail has a distinctive white tip. Being nocturnal, they rest during the day in antbear holes or in thickets and are not often seen.

DIET

Primarily scavengers; diet also includes reptiles, rodents, insects and wild fruits. Dependent on water. Unlike the black-backed jackal, they do not prey on livestock.

FAECES

They are almost identical to the black-backed jackal.

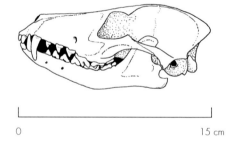

0   15 cm

0   5 cm

This species has an overall greyish appearance, lacking the saddle of the black-backed jackal.

—————— S P O O R ——————

Approximately 5 cm long. Identical to that of the black-backed jackal.

Actual size

Striped Polecat
Ictonyx striatus

Also called: Zorilla, Cape polecat, African skunk.
Afrikaans: Stinkmuishond   **Zulu:** Qaqa, Ngankakazana
Shona: Ehidembo   **Ndebele:** Iqaqa   **Tswana:** Nakedi
Venda: Thuri   **Transvaal Sotho:** Nakedi
Siswati: Licaca   **Lozi:** Kangamba   **Nama/Damara:** !Ūrob

---
DESCRIPTION

LENGTH: 70 cm   **SHOULDER HEIGHT:** 10 cm   **MASS:** 1,3 kg   **GESTATION:** 36 days.
The striped polecat is found singly or in pairs and is widely distributed. Nocturnal, it rests during the day in holes in the ground, in rocky crevices and in dense bush. It is a handsome animal with black and white vertical markings and a well-bushed tail. It is capable of shamming death, and when angered or cornered retaliates by ejecting a powerful, vile scent from the anal glands. Anything getting in the way of this secretion will carry the smell for days. The voice is a high-pitched scream. This useful creature – it has a preference for rodents – is best left alone.

DIET

Rodents, reptiles, insects, birds, frogs. Fond of poultry and adept at killing snakes.

FAECES

Light in colour; contorted in shape.

```
0                              5 cm
```

SPOOR
---

3 cm long; claws are well defined.

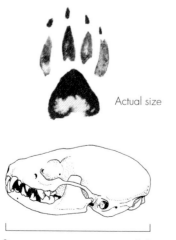

Actual size

```
0                    5,5 cm
```

Striped polecat

Striped Weasel
Poecilogale albinucha

Also called: Snake Weasel, White-naped Weasel
Afrikaans: Slangmuishond   **Zulu:** Nyengelezi

DESCRIPTION

OVERALL LENGTH: 50 cm   **SHOULDER HEIGHT:** 7 cm   **MASS:** 0,3 kg
GESTATION: 33–37 days.

More slender and lighter than the striped polecat, the striped weasel also ejects an evil-smelling fluid from the anal glands when threatened. Little else is known about this nocturnal species. It occurs singly or in pairs, and excavates its own burrow. The call includes a quiet growl or high-pitched growls uttered in rapid succession. The striped weasel appears to be fairly widespread in the eastern parts of southern Africa, and also occurs in Zimbabwe and Namibia.

DIET
Predominantly rodents and reptiles.

FAECES
Not collected.

SPOOR
Narrower than that of the polecat and about 1 cm shorter. The claws are not as well defined.

Actual size

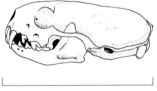

0   5 cm

Striped weasel

Honey Badger
Mellivora capensis

Afrikaans: Ratel   **Shona:** Sere, Tsere   **Ndebele:** Ulinda
Zulu, Siswati: Nsele   **Tswana:** Matswani, Matshwane
Venda: Tshiselele   **Shangaan:** Shidzidzi
Transvaal Sotho: Magôgê   **Lozi:** Sikape
Yei: Umbuli   **Nama/Damara:** | Harebab, | Hareseb

DESCRIPTION

LENGTH: 80 cm   **SHOULDER HEIGHT:** 26 cm   **MASS:** 9–12 kg
GESTATION: Approximately 180 days.

Widely distributed in southern Africa, honey badgers are fearless, display considerable aggression and have a powerful bite. Their loose skin enables them to turn easily upon anything that attempts to take hold of them. They will also turn and attack humans and vehicles and are therefore best left alone. Honey badgers are good at digging and, like the mongoose, are fond of digging out hardened dung beetle balls in search of larvae. These nocturnal creatures live in holes where, usually, they lie up during the day. Their sense of smell is acute.

DIET

Wide and varied diet, including reptiles, insects, larvae of dung beetles, eggs, ground birds, wild fruit, scorpions, grubs and wild honey. Also fond of poultry.

The honey badger has an interesting relationship with the greater honeyguide. In the Okavango Delta the call of the honeyguide can lead trackers directly to a beehive in the trunk of a mopane tree. In the same way, the honey badger follows the call of the greater honeyguide to the hive. The honey badger's tough hide is impervious to bee stings and it eats its fill, enjoying both honey and larvae. The honeyguide eats any leftover larvae and beeswax that its system can digest.

FAECES

Compact, dog-like in appearance.
Collected in the Okavango.

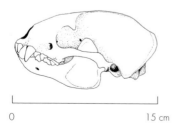

0					15 cm

0					5 cm

A honey badger digs out hardened dung beetle balls in search of larvae.

—————— S P O O R ——————

Forefoot long and broad, 5,5 cm; hind foot shorter; nail marks extended from the sole.

Hind foot

Actual size

Hollowed-out dung beetle balls.

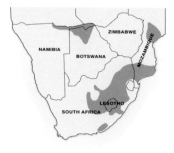

Spotted-necked Otter

Lutra maculicollis

Afrikaans: Kleinotter
Siswati: Ntsini   **Zulu:** Ntini   **Tswana:** Lenyebi
Lozi: Nibi   **Yei:** Ungwanda

DESCRIPTION

OVERALL LENGTH: 96 cm   **MASS:** 5 kg   **GESTATION:** 60 days.

Little is known of this diurnal mammal. It is found singly or in small groups and inhabits swamps, streams, backwaters of perennial rivers, and lakes, creating channels through the vegetation leading to the water's edge. This species is more aquatic by nature than the Cape clawless otter. Its distribution includes the Eastern Cape, KwaZulu-Natal and Swaziland. The most common call is a squeak or twittering.

DIET

Crabs, fish, frogs and aquatic insects. The snout or padded hands are used to probe into holes or under stones in search of food.

FAECES

Conspicuous latrine. Faeces contain fragments of shell from crabs and fish.

```
L__|__|__|__|__|
0              5 cm
```

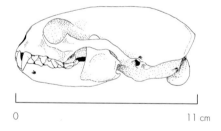

```
L_____|
0                          11 cm
```

The spotted-necked otter creates channels through the vegetation leading to the water's edge.

SPOOR

They have webbed toes armed with short, sharp claws.

Forefoot showing webbed toes.

Actual size

Cape Clawless Otter

Aonyx capensis

Afrikaans: Groototter **Shona:** Mbiti **Ndebele:** Intini
Zulu: Ntini **Siswati:** Ntsini **Venda:** Nivho
Tswana: Lenyebi, Nyedi **Lozi:** Mbao **Yei:** Utungwa
Nama/Damara: ‖ Gam, ǀ hareseb, ‖ Gamharebab

DESCRIPTION

OVERALL LENGTH: 1,4 m **MASS:** 22 kg **GESTATION:** 60–65 days.
These gregarious, robust otters are nocturnal as well as diurnal to some extent. Cape clawless otters do not confine themselves to water and wander some distance inland in search of food. They are excellent swimmers and their resting places are to be found amongst thick vegetation alongside the water, in hollows of tree roots and in crevices. These animals do not excavate burrows. They are well-developed and have an acute sense of smell and hearing. Widely distributed throughout Africa, the Cape clawless otter can be found in areas of permanent water.

DIET

Crabs, molluscs, fish, aquatic birds, rodents, frogs, small mammals and reptiles.

FAECES

Larger and darker than that of the spotted-necked otter. Deposited in conspicuous middens.

0   5 cm

These otters are dependent on water.

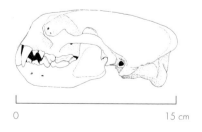

0   15 cm

62

At home in the water but somewhat clumsy on land.

The hind feet are partially webbed and the forefeet clawless; 7–8 cm long.

Small nails on the toes give it a clawless appearance.

Actual size

African Civet
Civettictis civetta

Afrikaans: Siwetkat **Shona:** Bvungo **Ndebele:** Insimba
Venda: Dhatshatsha, Dzamatamanga
Northern Sotho: Tsaparangaka **Tswana:** Tshipalore
Siswati: Lifungwe **Shangaan:** Fungwe
Lozi: Nyangongo **Nama/Damara:** !Noreb

DESCRIPTION

SHOULDER HEIGHT: 40 cm **MASS:** 18 kg
GESTATION: About 60 days; up to 4 young born during the summer months.
Civets are widespread in their distribution and common in the region. They are attractive and very distinctive animals, spotted on the body with stripes on the legs and on the bushy tail. Secretive and nocturnal, civets lie up during the day in tall grass, bush reed beds and holes in the ground. They are good swimmers. The cry is a low growl or a loud cough. When excited, they secrete an oily, tar-like substance from the peri-anal glands.

DIET

Mainly carnivorous. Snakes, rodents, birds, insects, millipedes, sun spiders, small mammals, fruits, other vegetable matter and berries. Fond of poultry and will raid camp kitchens in the bush. As with genets, one is well advised to lock away food-stuffs. They wander over great distances when feeding.

FAECES

Large for such an animal. Defecate in middens, often on high vantage points. Faeces easily recognized by the presence of millipede exoskeletons.

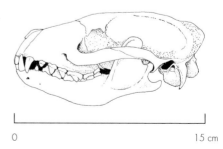

0   15 cm

The face shows a distinct black mark and white muzzle.

A circular track with nails clearly evident; 4 cm long.

Actual size

Large- & Small-spotted
Genets
Genetta tigrina/Genetta genetta

Afrikaans: Grootkolmuskeljaatkat en Kleinkolmuskeljaatkat
Siswati: Insimba **Tswana:** Tshipa **Lozi:** Sipa **Yei:** Unsiimba
Nama/Damara: !Noreb **Shona, Venda:** Tsimba
Ndebele: Insimba **Shangaan:** Nsimba **Sotho:** Tshipa

DESCRIPTION

LENGTH: 90 cm **MASS:** 2–3 kg **GESTATION:** About 70 days.
Genets are widely distributed, nocturnal and equally at home on the ground or climbing trees. Mainly solitary, they are bold and skilled poultry thieves. The large-spotted genet has a black-tipped tail whilst that of the small-spotted genet is white. The large-spotted genet is rusty coloured and is also known as the rusty-spotted genet.

DIET

Rodents, reptiles, insects, birds, frogs and wild fruits. Fond of poultry and will raid camp kitchens in the bush.

FAECES

Droppings are deposited at latrine sites which are usually in conspicuous places.

LARGE–SPOTTED   SMALL–SPOTTED

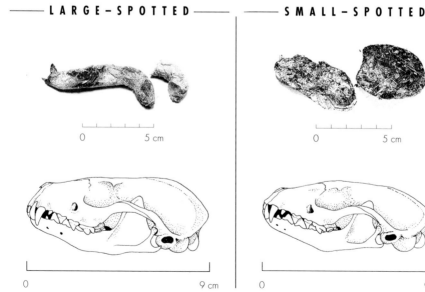

0   5 cm   0   5 cm

0   9 cm   0   9 cm

The large-spotted genet (top) and the small-spotted genet (bottom).

─────────── **S P O O R** ───────────
Similar for both species; 3 cm long.

Actual size

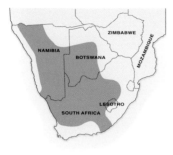

Suricate
Suricata suricatta

Afrikaans: Stokstertmeerkat   **Southern Sotho:** Toli
Transvaal Sotho: Letoto   **Tswana:** Kôtôkô/Sie
Nama/Damara: Xarab, !Naixarab

DESCRIPTION

LENGTH: 45 cm   **MASS:** 0,62–0,97 kg   **GESTATION:** About 60–70 days.
Suricates are highly sociable and live in large colonies. They excavate their own burrows but also utilize the burrows of the ground squirrel. Suricates are entirely diurnal and their natural enemies are the large raptors. Fond of sitting on their haunches and chattering, they often stand fully upright. They are small, compact animals with dark bands across the back, eye patches and a short tail with a black tip.

DIET

Insects, small birds and to a lesser extent, small mammals, the eggs of ground birds and reptiles. Food is obtained by digging with the claws of the forefeet. Water requirements are satisfied by the intake of roots, tubers and wild melons.

FAECES

Compact, small droppings comprising a variety of matter.

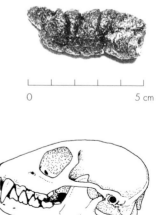

SPOOR

Compact and neat with conspicuous, long claws on the forefeet.

0   5 cm

Actual size

0   7 cm

A familiar pose of the suricate, although these animals frequently sit on their haunches.

Meller's Mongoose
Rhynchogale melleri

Afrikaans: Meller se Muishond

DESCRIPTION

LENGTH: 80 cm **MASS:** 2,7 kg.

It frequents forested savanna and is found in Mpumalanga, Mozambique and Zimbabwe. This is a fairly large mongoose, not unlike Selous' mongoose in shape and size, with a long, dark, white-tipped bushy tail and coarse, grey body hair. A solitary and nocturnal (occasionally diurnal) creature of which little is known.

DIET

Mainly termites; also small vertebrates.

FAECES

Almost impossible to distinguish faeces of one mongoose from that of another, except the water mongoose. All have a strong odour.

0   5 cm

SPOOR

Fairly elongated.

Hind Foot

Actual size

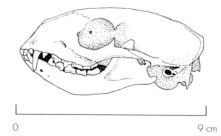

0   9 cm

Selous' Mongoose

Paracynictis selousi

Afrikaans: Kleinwitstertmuishond   **Shona:** Jerenyenje
Zulu: Nsengane   **Ndebele:** Duhwa, I(bu) Chakide
Tswana: Kgano   **Nama/Damara:** !Uri ǂ are ǂ ao | ēb

DESCRIPTION

LENGTH: 70 cm overall   **SHOULDER HEIGHT:** 20 cm   **MASS:** Up to 2,7 kg.
Nocturnal and found singly or in pairs, Selous' mongoose has long curved claws adapted for digging. Unlike other mongooses, it dig tunnels which interlink to form burrows. It is widespread in Zimbabwe although uncommon in the Northern Province and Mpumalanga in South Africa, and Botswana, Namibia and Angola.

DIET

Insects, larvae, small rodents, birds.

FAECES

Strong odour. Similar to faeces of other mongooses.

SPOOR

Distinctive curved claws; four toes to each foot.

Actual size

```
|__|__|__|__|__|
0                5 cm
```

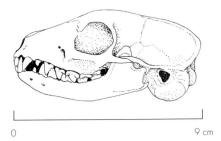

```
|_____|
0                        9 cm
```

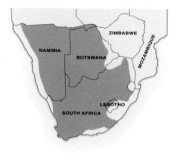

Yellow Mongoose

Cynictis penicillata

Other names: Bushy-tailed Mongoose
Afrikaans: Rooimeerkat, Geelmuishond
Tswana: Ramoswe, Motodi **Transvaal Sotho:** Pipi
Nama/Damara: | Apa | ēb

DESCRIPTION

LENGTH: 50–65 cm **GESTATION:** Unknown.

Generally diurnal, the yellow mongoose is endemic to southern Africa. It lives in colonies in open country in the Cape, Free State, the North-West Province and Northern Province of South Africa and Namibia. It is absent in most of KwaZulu-Natal. It is fond of burrowing. The coat is long and yellowish brown in colour, and the ears are fairly large. Figures are not available on this species' mass, but it is a small mongoose with a short, pointed muzzle and a short, white-tipped tail.

DIET

Termites, but mostly insects, frogs, birds, rodents and other vertebrates.

SPOOR

3 cm long.

FAECES

Similar to that of other mongooses with a strong odour. Deposited in latrines and at the entrance to burrows.

Actual size

0 |___|___|___|___|___| 5 cm

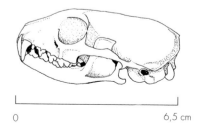

0   6,5 cm

A yellow mongoose stands erect to survey the landscape for any danger.

Small Grey Mongoose

Galerella pulverulenta

Afrikaans: Kaapse grysmuishond

DESCRIPTION

LENGTH: 55–70 cm **MASS:** 0,7–0,9 kg **GESTATION:** Not known.

A diurnal, terrestrial mongoose, found singly, in pairs or in small family groups. It is shy and elusive and more stockily built than the slender mongoose. The general colour is mottled grey as the hairs are ringed black and white. This species is common in the Cape south of the Orange River.

DIET

Fruit, rodents, amphibians, snakes, lizards, birds and their eggs, hares, insects.

FAECES

Similar to faeces of other mongooses, with a strong odour.

```
0          5 cm
```

SPOOR

Not collected or observed.

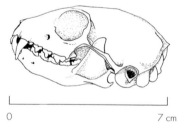

```
0                7 cm
```

The small grey mongoose forages during daylight hours only.

White-tailed Mongoose

Ichneumia albicauda

Afrikaans: Witstertmuishond **Xhosa:** Ngqwalashu
Zulu: Gqalashu **Ndebele:** Ubachakide **Shona:** Jerenyenje
Tswana: Leselamotlhaba, Tshagane **Venda:** Mutsherere
Shangaan: Tlolota **Siswati:** Liduha

DESCRIPTION

LENGTH: 1,2 m **SHOULDER HEIGHT:** 25 cm **MASS:** 3–5 kg.
Mainly nocturnal and solitary, this mongoose frequents rivers, marshes, vleis and
well-bushed areas. It will wander fair distances from water in search of food. During
the day it rests in holes and cavities. It is darkish grey in colour with darker under-
parts and a white tip to the tail.

DIET

Mainly insects and other invertebrates as well as poultry, frogs, carrion, crabs,
rodents, birds, fish, reptiles, berries and fruits.

SPOOR

Five toes to forefeet and hind feet with
long curved claws, the tips of which are
conspicuous; 4 cm long.

FAECES

Similar to other mongoose faeces.
Strong odour.

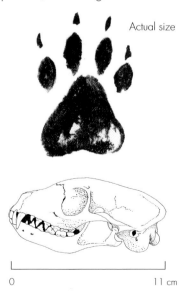

Actual size

0   5 cm

0   11 cm

A nocturnal mongoose, generally solitary.

75

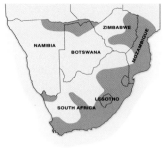

Water Mongoose

Atilax paludinosus

Afrikaans: Kommetjiegatmuishond   **Shona:** Chidzvororo
Ndebele: Imvuzi   **Xhosa:** Vuzi   **Zulu:** Mvuzi
Tswana: Tshagane   **Sotho:** Motswitswi   **Siswati:** Liduha
Lozi: Mukala   **Yei:** Ugwagara

DESCRIPTION

LENGTH: 70 cm   **SHOULDER HEIGHT:** 15 cm   **MASS:** 5 kg.

These solitary animals are adept at digging. They are good swimmers and have well-developed cheek teeth for crushing crabs and beetles. Water mongooses emit a strong scent from the anal gland when disturbed, or to mark their territories. They have a short tapering tail and a robust, dark brown body.

DIET

Crabs, fish, reptiles, insects, rodents, birds and wild fruit. They are reputed to prey on the eggs of the crocodile.

FAECES

Found in middens at the water's edge; faeces contain remains of shells and have a strong odour, like most of the other mongooses.

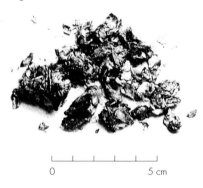

0   5 cm

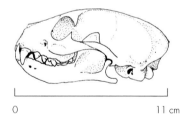

0   11 cm

A large dark brown, long-haired mongoose associated with fresh water and also coastal edges.

SPOOR

Pointed toes, well adapted to searching for prey underwater; 4 cm long.

Actual size

Large Grey Mongoose
Herpestes ichneumon

Afrikaans: Grootgrysmuishond **Zulu:** Nhlangala
Tswana: Leswekete, Tshagane

---------- **DESCRIPTION** ----------

LENGTH: 1 m **MASS:** 3–4 kg **GESTATION:** About 60 days.
The species name, *ichneumon*, comes from the Greek word for 'tracker'; it is a never-tiring hunter of mainly small vertebrates. A diurnal species found singly or in pairs, it swims well and favours riverine vegetation such as reed beds. It is entirely terrestrial and has a widespread distribution. It is grey in colour with a black tip to the tail, and a blackish face and feet. Usually frequents water.

---------- **DIET** ----------

Fish, crabs, birds, rodents, reptiles, insects and fruit.

---------- **FAECES** ----------

Similar to other mongoose faeces, with a strong odour.

---------- **SPOOR** ----------

Elongated with pointed claws; spoor 4 cm long.

0   5 cm

Actual size

0   10 cm

Slender Mongoose

Galerella sanguinea

Other name: Black-tipped mongoose.
Afrikaans: Rooimuishond **Zulu:** Chakide **Siswati:** Chakidze
Venda: Khohe **Shona:** Hovo **Ndebele:** Iwobo **Tswana:**
Ramotsibodis, Kganwe **Sotho:** Kgano **Shangaan:** Mangovo

─────────── **DESCRIPTION** ───────────

LENGTH: 60 cm (including tail) **SHOULDER HEIGHT:** 13 cm **MASS:** 5 kg
GESTATION: About 45 days.

This diurnal, solitary species has a wide habitat tolerance, and is not dependent on water. It is terrestrial, but will take to trees when in search of birds' eggs. It is preyed upon by raptors. Like most mongooses it is prone to rabies. The tail has a distinctive black tip. Another form, *Galerella sanguinea nigrata*, from the Kunene Province, Namibia, is dark with a broad black line on the back and a black-tipped tail.

─────────── **DIET** ───────────

Snakes, rodents, insects, scorpions. An aggressive hunter capable of dispatching mamba and other dangerous snakes. A notorious thief of young poultry.

─────── **FAECES** ───────

Similar to faeces of other mongooses, with a strong odour.

─────── **SPOOR** ───────

Forefeet claws sharp and curved. Neat, narrow track, about 3 cm long.

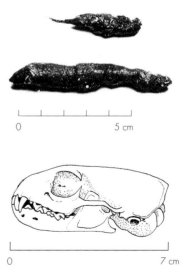

0   5 cm

Actual size

0   7 cm

Banded Mongoose

Mungos mungo

Afrikaans: Gebande muishond
Ndebele: Usikibhoror **Shona:** Dzvoro **Tswana:** Letototo
Venda: Tshihoho **Shanqaan:** Nkala **Zulu:** Buhala
Lozi: Kaâalañâti

--- **DESCRIPTION** ---

LENGTH: 60 cm **SHOULDER HEIGHT:** 13 cm **MASS:** 1,5 kg **GESTATION:** 60 days.
Banded mongooses are inquisitive and gregarious and found in groups of up to 40 individuals. Diurnal, they live in antbear or termite holes or in holes they dig themselves. When attacked by predator birds they defend themselves vigorously. They have well-developed senses. Like most mongooses, they are adept at killing snakes. They frequently stand on their hind legs to obtain a better view. A distinguishing feature is the distinctive bands that run from the shoulders to the base of the tail.

--- **DIET** ---

Primarily insects. Beetle larvae form a favourite part of their diet and dung beetle balls are a prime target. Also eat rodents, snails, roots, wild fruit, reptiles, scorpions, and birds' eggs, which they break open by rolling it through their hind legs against rocks. Noisy when feeding.

--- **FAECES** ---

Similar to other mongooses, with a strong odour.

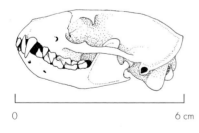

0   6 cm

0   5 cm

This diurnal and very gregarious species lives in groups of up to 40 individuals.

Foreclaws twice as long as the hind claws which are 3 cm long.

Actual size

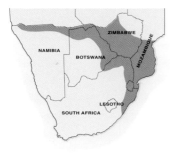

Dwarf Mongoose
Helogale parvula

Afrikaans: Dwergmuishond
Sotho: Motswitswane
Ndebele: Iduha **Venda:** Matswi

DESCRIPTION

LENGTH: 40 cm **SHOULDER HEIGHT:** 7 cm **MASS:** 0,3 kg **GESTATION:** 45–50 days.
The smallest of the African mongooses, these diurnal creatures live in large family groups in antbear holes, old logs, rock crevices or old burrows. The pack is led by the senior female; together with the dominant male she forms the breeding pair. These mammals are bold and tireless in their search for food. The body colour is dark brown to almost black, especially from a distance. Like other mongooses, they utter sharp alarm calls and sit up on their hind legs when disturbed. Dwarf mongooses fall prey to larger predators, raptors and snakes, and are likely to contract rabies. Very agile, they climb and jump well, and move at a fast, scurrying pace.

DIET

They will eat virtually anything: insects, grubs, rodents, wild fruit, eggs. Independent of water.

SPOOR

Small track, about 2 cm long showing sharp, long claws; soles of feet are naked to the heel.

FAECES

Deposited at the entrance to homes; often composed of finely ground insects.

Actual size

L____I____I____I____I
0   5 cm

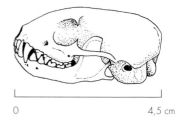

L_____I
0   4,5 cm

A diurnal species found in family groups often in abandoned termite mounds.

Aardwolf
Proteles cristatus

Shona: Mwena **Ndebele:** Inthuhu **Venda:** Tshivingwi
Xhosa, Zulu: Nehi **Siswati:** Ngci **Tswana:** Thukwi, Mmabudu
Lozi: Mutosi **Yei:** Unshushi **Nama/Damara:** Gīb

DESCRIPTION

SHOULDER HEIGHT: 50 cm **MASS:** Up to 11 kg **GESTATION:** 60 days.

Aardwolves have fairly long, but weak, canine teeth; there is no evidence available to suggest that they prey on livestock. Timid and inoffensive, they occur singly or in pairs. As they are nocturnal, they lie up during the day in burrows which they excavate, or in disused antbear holes. If disturbed and excited, they emit a strong odour from the anal glands. The emission is not as strong, however, as that of the striped polecat. Secretions from the anal gland are also used to mark territories, the pasting usually done on a grass stalk. Their habitat includes desert plains and thornveld. The voice is a dog-like bark, but these animals are also capable of roaring.

DIET

Feed mainly on termites. Will occasionally also feed on small rodents, beetles, bugs, ants and millipedes.

FAECES

Large in comparison to animal's size. Covered with sand in latrines. A large proportion of the scat is pure sand, taken in whilst licking up termites.

0   5 cm

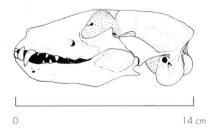

0   14 cm

A highly specialized carnivore adapted to feeding on termites.

Not unlike that of a hyaena but less than half the length. Four toes on the forelegs and five on the hind legs.

Actual size

Spotted Hyaena

Crocuta crocuta

Afrikaans: Gevlekte hiëna **Xhosa, Zulu, Siswati, Sindebele:** Mpisi **Shangaan:** Mhisi **Sotho, Tswana:** Phiri **Shona:** Bere **Venda:** Phele **Lozi:** Sitongwani **Yei:** Umpuru **Nama/Damara:** Gara ǂ hiras

DESCRIPTION

SHOULDER HEIGHT: 70–90 cm **MASS:** 50–85 kg **GESTATION:** 105 days; 2–3 young.
Found throughout the African savanna, spotted hyaena are noisy animals with a variety of calls, moans, laughs and shrieks. They both scavenge and hunt, feeding on anything they find. The jaws are powerful, capable even of cracking the leg bones of a giraffe. Primarily nocturnal creatures, they emerge from antbear holes, caves and rocky areas at nightfall. In areas where they are not hunted by man they can be seen during daylight hours. They possess excellent sight, hearing and sense of smell. Although cunning, powerful and treacherous, spotted hyaena show a fear of lions and wild dogs.

When camping out in the open at night, caution must be exercised and foodstuffs (particularly meat) should not be left lying about. If you are sleeping under the stars, it is advisable to keep a good fire going and to mount night watches. They can become extremely bold when hungry; there have been cases of sleeping people losing parts of their faces to these animals. These swift animals are capable of speeds of up to 45 km/h. They are found singly, in pairs, or in groups of up to 30 at a kill.

They are observant and watch vultures descending on a kill; they also follow lions calling. They have distinct territories, but clan structures overlap with varying degrees of tolerance. The females are larger than the males and dominate the pack. The spotted hyaena is not dependent on water but will drink regularly when water is available. The undertakers of the African savanna, these interesting animals deserve a better understanding and much more is yet to be learnt about them.

DIET

Carnivorous; both predator and scavenger. Will eat large quantities of bone without difficulty.

Spotted hyaena have strong teeth and jaws.

High shoulders with sloping hindquarters characterize the spotted hyaena.

FAECES

Green in colour when fresh, faeces turn pure white with age because of their mineral and bone content. Conspicuous latrine areas are usually found in open areas; they also urinate at regular places. Faeces consisting entirely of hair are common, and vomit consisting of hair, bone fragments and hooves is occasionally found.

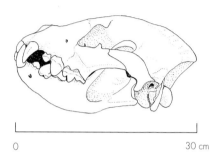

0   30 cm

SPOOR

Much like that of a large dog and identical to that of the brown hyaena but only larger. Broad in the main pad of the forefoot. Claw tips are distinctly visible; hind foot is distinctly smaller than the forefoot.

11 cm long

Hyaena will readily feed on the remains of any dead animal which they come across.

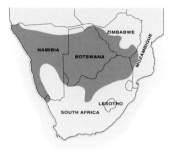

Brown Hyaena
Hyaena brunnea

Afrikaans: Strandjut   **Ndebele:** Impisi   **Shona:** Bere
Sotho: Phirbjokwane   **Tswana:** Tlonkana, Phiritshwana
Bushman: Nutsa   **Nama/Damara:** ǂ Hiras

DESCRIPTION

SHOULDER HEIGHT: 71–81 cm   **MASS:** 50–56 kg   **GESTATION:** 90 days; 2–3 young.
Recent studies have revealed the species to be more abundant than previously believed. It is a shy, nocturnal animal that lies up in antbear holes by day. It is well adapted to the dry regions of southern Africa and areas devoid of surface water. Like the spotted hyaena, this species has a well-developed digestive system and an efficient olfactory system for locating carrion. It is found in Zimbabwe, Angola, Botswana, Namibia, and in South Africa in the North-West Province, Northern Province, Gauteng, Eastern Province and the Northern Cape across to the Atlantic Ocean. Far more silent than the spotted hyaena, the brown hyaena utters resonant 'whoofs'. The distinctive laugh of the spotted hyaena is absent. It gives lion a wide berth and is totally dominated by the spotted hyaena.

DIET

Wide and varied; includes insects, birds, eggs, wild fruits, springhares, domestic stock, antelope and carrion (scavenged vertebrate remains). Along the coast of Namibia and the Northern Cape Province, it feeds on the washed-up remains of marine animals from which it acquired the name 'strandjut'. During the dry winter months it forages for up to 12 hours at night.

FAECES

Green when fresh, turns white with age. Defecates at latrine areas. Paste secretions can be found on grass stalks.

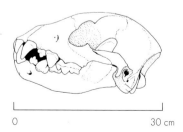

0   30 cm

Brown hyaena have a distinct dark brown shaggy coat and erect, pointed ears.

SPOOR

Dog-like with short, blunt claws. Protected species, but more common than believed due to its silent nature and nocturnal habits.

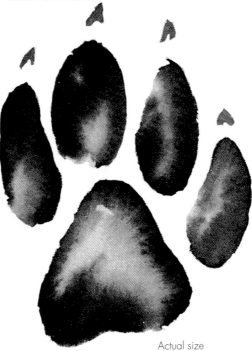

Actual size

Lion
Panthera leo

Afrikaans: Leeu **Shona:** Shumba **Ndebele:** Isilwane
Zulu: Ngonyama **Siswati:** Ngwenyama **Shangaan:** Nghala,
N'shumba **Sotho, Lozi, Tswana:** Tau **Venda:** Ndau
Yei: Undavu **Nama/Damara:** Xammi

--- **D E S C R I P T I O N** ---

SHOULDER HEIGHT: 91–120 cm **MASS:** males 181–227 kg, females 113–152 kg
GESTATION: About 102 days; breed throughout the year.

Lions are both diurnal and nocturnal. They are highly social animals and are found in small prides and groups of up to 20 individuals. They prey on a wide range of species, including small rodents, and have excellent sight, hearing and sense of smell. One may, however, come across a lion when heading into a stiff wind or stumble on a pack of sleeping lions.

So much has been written about lions that one risks repetition. For the benefit of those who might encounter lions on foot, however the following significant observations should be noted.

Should you encounter lions, remain absolutely still – under *no* circumstances run. Issue this instruction to other members of the party before you set off into the bush.

A lioness with cubs may charge if she is given a fright or feels threatened. I had an experience where my trackers shouted at a lioness and halted her within five metres of us. The continual shouting caused her to lose her nerve and she backed off.

Males more often than not 'bluff'; in all my encounters with males they have always fled. Wounded lions, male or female, are a different proposition for they become highly aggressive and dangerous.

When a lion is about to charge, it lashes its tail up and down, flattens its ears, and roars simultaneously. It runs slowly and then more swiftly, somewhat crouched, with the head held low and the tail erect and stiff. In this situation it is

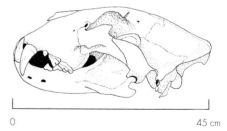

0   45 cm

very difficult to remain still. One's inherent desire is to flee, but this carries with it the certainty of a permanent end to lion-watching.

If you are in charge of a party and you encounter a lioness that does not back off and run away, instruct your group, once you have assessed her reaction, to back away slowly until out of sight. Although you might be suitably armed, your chances of hitting a charging lion are remote, so discretion under these circumstances would be the better part of valour. Avoid thickets and dense, tall grass in the first place.

The largest and most imposing of all the African carnivores.

Keep a large fire going while camping out at night and mount a watch for added protection; lions are notoriously bold. The Bayei of the Okavango will not camp on Chiefs Island and give lions resident in the area a wide berth at night.

Both males and females roar as a means of communication and territorial demarcation. As a rule lions are silent when hunting, usually filling the night air with deep roars only after a successful kill. They call at dawn, to locate each other, especially after hunting. The vocal calls range from a deep roar to low, soft, moaning coughs.

Lions are extremely powerful and they are very good jumpers and swimmers. Their powerful claws are fully retractable like those of all true cats. They hunt by sight and sound rather than by scent; females are the principal killers. Hunting is always conducted in a cooperative, intelligent manner, either in groups or singly. Lions are at the top of the food chain and have no natural enemies – man is actually their greatest enemy and threat.

Mortality in young lions up to two years of age is high. Fights among older members, accidents during hunting and disease in lions in poor condition account for most deaths. Lions are still common throughout the national parks, reserves and bushveld regions of southern Africa. An ever-increasing threat to the survival of these animals is the robbing of kills by man in search of food.

DIET

Lions will eat virtually anything when hungry, including carrion. Usually they prey on medium-hoofed to large-hoofed animals. In the Okavango they pull down lone buffalo bulls and bulls on the outskirts of herds. Giraffe also fall prey to these cats although the lion is mindful of their savage kick. Lion have been observed feeding on a crocodile on the banks of the Luangwa River, Zambia. They hunt, in the main, at night. Lions drink regularly when water is available, though they are capable of going without water for long periods in deserts and arid areas. The Kalahari lions have been observed eating *tsamma* melons and gemsbok cucumbers.

Two male lions resting.

FAECES

Similar to that of the leopard, but larger. When lions have consumed a fair amount of blood, the dung is usually very black and strong-smelling. Turns white when there is a high calcium content. Hair is passed without other matter being present and sometimes faeces may consist of bundles of porcupine quills.

Lion faeces encrusted with porcupine quills.

0   5 cm

Unmistakable, large pug marks. In spite of their size, they tread lightly. Claws are fully sheathed.

12 cm

Leopard
Panthera pardus

Afrikaans: Luiperd   **Zulu, Ndebele, Siswati, Xhosa, Shangaan, Tsonga, Venda:** Ngwe, Ingwe   **Herero, Ovambo:** Ngwi   **Tswana, Sotho:** Nkwe, Inkwe   **Lozi:** Ngwe   **Yei:** Ungwe   **Nama/Damara:** | Garub

---
DESCRIPTION

SHOULDER HEIGHT: 70 cm   **MASS:** 60–80 kg   **GESTATION:** 105 days.

Leopards are shy, solitary creatures – cunning and far more silent than lions. They climb expertly and are found in a wide range of habitats from dense forest to mountains, bushveld and desert. They are less easily seen on foot than any other carnivore, and most dangerous when wounded, cornered or persistently disturbed. The call is a coughing, rasping sound. Hunted for their pelts, their numbers have been heavily reduced, although they are probably more common than generally believed. They usually kill their prey by biting through the throat and nape of the neck. Large kills are hauled into the fork of a tree out of the reach of lions, wild dogs, hyaenas and vultures. After disemboweling the prey, they feed on the chest, thighs or around the anus. They lap blood readily which satisfies their moisture requirements.

DIET

Carnivorous. Diverse diet, ranging from insects to domestic stock. Includes fish, reptiles, birds, dassies, dogs and decaying flesh. They are partial to baboons and will venture to the topmost branches of a tree in an attempt to corner one. Impala are considered to form the principal part of their diet in savanna and bush ecosystems where leopard are common. Leopard are not dependent on water, but will drink when water is available.

FAECES

Smaller than the lion; occasionally turns white in colour and often contain a high percentage of fur.

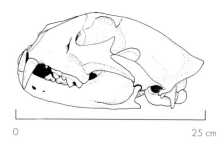

0   25 cm

Leopards are solitary, secretive and mainly nocturnal animals.

Smaller and more compact than that of the lion. Neat, round impression in soft sand or mud; tread is very light. Overall gait is 95–100 cm.

6,5–9 cm

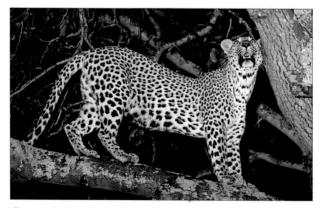

Expert climbers, leopards can drag fairly large prey up into trees.

Scrape marks

One of the most graceful of all the cats.

The whiskers are long and white, rising from dark spots on the muzzle.

Cheetah
Acinonyx jubatus

Afrikaans: Jagluiperd **Ndebele, Zulu:** Ihlosi, Hlosi
Shangaan: Khankankha **Tswana, Sotho:** Lengau
Venda: Dagaladzhie **Herero:** Shitona **Ovambo:** Shinga
Siswati: Lihlosi **Lozi:** Linau **Yei:** Unqaba
Nama/Damara: !Arub

DESCRIPTION

SHOULDER HEIGHT: 75 cm MASS: 55–59 kg GESTATION: 90–95 days; litter 2–4.
Cheetah are both diurnal and nocturnal. Records from Etosha and the Kalahari confirm their nocturnal habits.

These cats rely on their considerable speed over short distances of up to 400 metres when hunting. The long legs have non-retractable claws which provide an additional grip on the ground and aid their swift, sideways, jinking movements. Hunting is also aided by excellent sight. This species is not dangerous to man. When encountered on foot, a cheetah will look long and hard in your direction and then move off at great speed. They can, however, be aggressive under captive conditions and it is always advisable to handle them with care. A whack in the face with those long claws will not easily be forgotten.

Mortality is high in cubs, which fall victim to lion, spotted hyaena, wild dogs and leopard, as well as to large eagles, within the first three months of being born. Adults are sometimes killed by lions. The numbers of cheetah are surprisingly low in areas with suitable prey, for example the Kruger National Park. Competition from other carnivores could be a limiting factor. Cheetah are found in a wide range of habitats although they prefer open grassland and light woodland. The voice is a chirping, bird-like call, with hissing and spitting, low growls and purring.

DIET

A carnivorous species. Preys on medium-sized antelope, guinea fowl, hares, springhares, porcupines, bustards and ostrich, and is prone to attack domestic stock. Prey is run down at considerable speed and often bowled over by having the hind legs knocked out from under it. Death is brought about by strangulation. It will not eat carrion or anything that has not been freshly killed. It is thought to be fairly independent of water, but will drink readily when water is available.

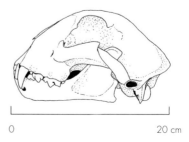

0   20 cm

Endangered species

Cheetah rely on excellent sight and speed for hunting.

Not unlike that of the leopard. Remain dark in colour.

————————————— **SPOOR** —————————————

Distinctive track clearly showing the claws which are non-retractable. A narrower track than that of the spotted hyaena, with toes more evenly spaced.

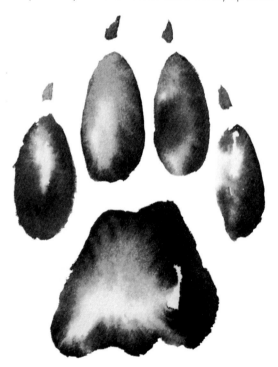

Actual size

Cheetah have a distinctive tear line running from the eye to the mouth.

Caracal
Felis caracal

Afrikaans: Rooikat **Xhosa:** Nghawa **Zulu:** Ndabushe
Sindebele: Ntwane **Tswana, Sotho:** Thwane **Venda:** Thwani
Shona: Hwang, Twana **Ndebele:** Indabutshe, Intwane
Siswati: Indabushe **Lozi:** Twani **Yei:** Shilizabula
Nama/Damara: !Hab, |Apa |hôab

DESCRIPTION

SHOULDER HEIGHT: 40 cm **MASS:** 16 kg **GESTATION:** 75 days; up to 2 kittens.
Like the serval the caracal is mainly nocturnal and solitary. It is shy, lying up during the day. If cornered it will savagely defend itself and spit loudly, otherwise it is silent. It will sometimes purr softly. This animal occurs widely but sparsely in most of southern Africa; it is rare in populated areas.

DIET

Carnivorous. Rats and mice make up the usual diet, but small mammals, such as dassies, monkeys and game birds are also eaten. This species is more powerful than the serval, taking larger prey up to the size of a young kudu. Also known to take full-grown sheep and goats. The prey is usually knocked down with a sideways slap; the serval uses a downward slap. It has been known to spring into the air to seize a low-flying bird.

FAECES

Occasionally turns white; contains hair and fine bone fragments. Fairly long faeces in relation to animal's size. Not deposited in same place and not covered.

0   5 cm

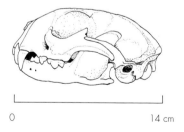

0   14 cm

The caracal is easily recognized by its long, tufted, black-tipped ears.

Similar to serval. 5–6 cm long.

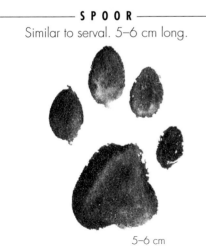

5–6 cm

Serval
Felis serval

Afrikaans: Tierboskat **Xhosa:** Hlosi, Ngwenkala
Zulu, Sindebele: Ndlozi **Siswati:** Indloti **Tswana:** Tadi
Venda: Didingwe **Southern Sotho:** Qoako, Phaha, Tholi
Shona: Nzudzi **Ndebele:** Inhlozi **Lozi:** Nwela **Yei:** Unqosile
Nama/Damara: !Garu !garo | hôab

DESCRIPTION

SHOULDER HEIGHT: 50 cm **MASS:** 10–14 kg
LENGTH: 71 cm (without tail); tail is 27 cm **GESTATION:** 75 days; 2–4 kittens
BREEDING: During the warmer months, August–February.

The serval is nocturnal and occurs alone or in pairs. It is a shy, retiring cat, hiding up during the day in reedbeds, tall grass and scrub bush. If pursued it will take to a tree, climbing with ease. The plaintive, high-pitched 'how-how-how' cry may be heard where the species is numerous. It is widespread and relatively common throughout southern Africa, except in the drier areas of Namibia, Botswana, the Free State and Cape and North-West provinces of South Africa. It is hunted mercilessly. There is no evidence of it feeding on domestic stock.

DIET

Carnivorous. Preys mainly on game birds and small mammals such as rodents and small antelope like the duiker. Possibly fish and vegetable matter are eaten as well. Has a tendency to raid poultry.

FAECES

Similar to the caracal in every aspect. Often contains a great deal of fur.

```
0                    5 cm
```

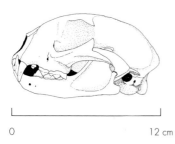

```
0                    12 cm
```

The serval resembles a small cheetah but has a short tail.

Similar to the caracal. 4–4,5 cm long.

4 cm

African Wild Cat
Felis lybica

Afrikaans: Vaalboskat **Shona:** Nhiriri **Ndebele:** Igola
Tswana: Phage **Shangaan:** Mphaha **Venda:** Phaha
Southern Sotho: Tsetse **Zulu:** Mpaka **Xhosa:** Ngada
Siswati: Imbodla **Lozi:** Sinono **Yei:** Uqhumu
Nama/Damara: !Garo | hôab

--- **DESCRIPTION** ---

SHOULDER HEIGHT: 35 cm **MASS:** 5–6 kg **GESTATION:** 56–60 days.
This is the cat of the ancient Egyptians who domesticated the species around 4 000 BC. The African wild cat is widespread in the region and has a wide habitat tolerance. Nocturnal and shy, it frequents tall grass and thick bush. This cat falls prey to the caracal, leopard and the larger birds of prey. The African wild cat cross-breeds with domestic cats. This is cause for concern as the species is becoming hybridized.

--- **DIET** ---

Varied. Poultry, rodents, birds, reptiles, insects, hares and wild fruits.

--- **FAECES** ---
Compact; often has a strong odour.

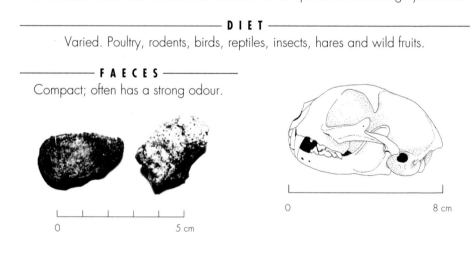

0   5 cm

0   8 cm

The African wild cat is very similar to the ordinary domestic cat in appearance.

———————— SPOOR ————————

Similar to the domestic cat; 3 cm long.

Actual size

Small Spotted Cat

Felis nigripes

Afrikaans: Kleingekoldekat **Southern Sotho:** Tsetse
Tswana: Sabalabolokwane **Nama/Damara:** ǂNu ǂaibeb

DESCRIPTION

SHOULDER HEIGHT: About 25 cm **MASS:** Up to 2 kg **GESTATION:** About 68 days.
Little is known of this small cat which is endemic to southern Africa. The small spotted cat makes up for its size by being extremely vicious: it attacks with its teeth and claws. These solitary and nocturnal cats take refuge in dense scrub or holes in the ground such as old termitaria.

DIET

Rats, mice, elephant shrews, ground squirrels, lizards and invertebrates such as spiders and insects, including beetles, grasshoppers and moths.

FAECES

Fairly large for such a small cat.

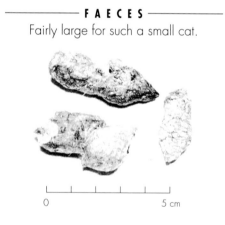

0   5 cm

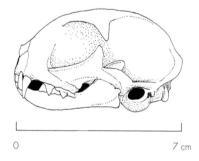

0   7 cm

The small spotted cat can be mistaken for the African wild cat but differs in size and colour.

———— SPOOR ————

Smaller track than that of the African wild cat.

Actual size

Aardvark
Orycteropus afer

Afrikaans: Erdvark **Shona:** Sambani **Ndebele:** Isambane
Zulu: Sambane **Shangaan:** Xombana **Tswana, Transvaal**
Sotho: Thakadu **Venda:** Thagalu **Siswati:** Sambane
Lozi: Takalo **Yei:** Ungengu **Nama/Damara:** | Khuwub

DESCRIPTION

OVERALL LENGTH: 1,5 m **SHOULDER HEIGHT:** 60 cm **MASS:** Up to 68 kg
GESTATION: 210 days; single young.

Nocturnal and solitary, aardvark are widely distributed throughout southern Africa. The flesh is greatly sought after by tribal Africans. These powerful animals are capable of digging at great speed. They dig their own burrows which later are used by porcupines, pythons, warthogs, jackals, hyaenas, leopards, wild dogs and wild cats as homes. Their senses of hearing and scent are well developed for finding their food source, termites, and for sensing the presence of predators. The leopard and the lion, particularly the latter, are their principal enemies. These animals are seldom seen, although reminders of their presence exist in the form of large holes which can be seen in the road when driving through the bush.

DIET

Almost exclusively termites. It uses its well-developed claws to dig into termite mounds, then inserts its 45 cm-long tongue to which the termites adhere. Has also been known to eat wild melons.

FAECES

Distinctive, oblong pellets almost completely made up of sand. Droppings are covered up.

SPOOR

Can be up to 9 cm long; the triple indentation of the hind foot is unmistakable when seen in the soil.

Unique in appearance, the aardvark is easily recognized by its long snout and elongated ears.

Forefoot
4–4,5 cm

Hind foot
8–9 cm

Elephant
Loxodonta africana

Afrikaans: Olifant Zulu, Siswati, Xhosa: Ndhlovu
Transvaal Shangaan, Tsanga: Ndlopfu
Motswana, Transvaal Sotho: Tlou Herero: Ndjou
Venda: Ndou Sindebele: Ndhlovu, Nkubu Shona: Nzou,
Zhou Lozi: Tou Yei: Unjovo Nama/Damara: ǂKhoab

DESCRIPTION

SHOULDER HEIGHT: 3 m MASS: Up to 6 000 kg. At birth the calf is 90 cm tall and weighs approximately 120 kg. Suckled until about 2 years old. GESTATION: 22 months; single calf. Twins have been recorded, but this is extremely rare. Breed throughout the year; one calf every 5 years or so. SPEED: 9–12 km/h. Storming at full charge, upwards of 40 km/h.

Elephants are essentially gregarious creatures by nature and may be found in groups of 10–20 or up to 50 and more. Massing of elephants in numbers in excess of 100 is usually caused by outside pressures, but may also occur at certain times of the year, especially towards the end of the dry season. Elephant behaviour, however, varies from area to area.

Elephants have a highly developed social structure and family units are led by a cow elephant or matriarch. The matriarch is, by natural selection, the most experienced member of th group and automatically assumes leadership. The composition of the herd varies and one will find bulls of various ages in attendance. A bull may be distinguished from a cow by its rounded forehead; the cow's forehead is angular. Both sexes have tusks. Bulls leave the family unit at puberty (10–12 years) and, in many instances, are driven out by the older cows.

FIELD OBSERVATIONS

One should always approach elephants with great caution. They have poor eyesight and hearing. The cows are normally nervous and will not hesitate to attack if they are disturbed, especially when with young. Bull elephants are far more tolerant than cows. When they do put on a threat display, they advance with ears held out like large sails and the head held slightly back. Thereafter they invariably turn aside with back arched and tail held high. Bulls do charge, but in most cases it is sheer bluff in order to scare one off.

Elephants are dangerous when wounded or when continously pursued, hunted or annoyed. They are incapable of moving on three legs and, when wounded in the knee, are totally helpless. Once, when I was leading a trail, a lone bull picked up our scent and proceeded to search for us. We retreated in as orderly a fashion as the circumstances would allow. Bulls usually can be driven off by throwing sand clods or wood onto the ground in front of them or by shouting and clapping one's

Elephants use their tusks for digging, probing for food and for fighting.

hands continuously. I once had to throw my *velskoen* at an over-inquisitive bull which, I feared, would lift our tents off the ground. These bulls invariably move off some distance and continue feeding.

Bulls on the fringe of breeding herds which take fright either by smelling you or by being disturbed by running impala, wildebeest or zebra, often alarm the whole herd by running towards it. Even warthogs cause a nervous reaction, mainly among young bulls. The presence of zebra and impala is the biggest obstacle when observing elephant. They have acute eyesight and tend to spot humans quickly, often running directly towards the elephant herd, thereby causing the herd to move off.

When approaching an elephant, move upwind and use every possible piece of cover that is available. Should an elephant stop feeding, either raising its head or with the grass or branch it is feeding on suspended in its mouth, remain absolutely still until the elephant resumes feeding. Move when it flaps its ears forward, a sign that it has not detected you. Although an elephant's eyesight is reputedly bad, it can still spot you and, therefore, when tracking elephants always avoid wearing white or light-coloured clothing.

DANGER SIGNALS

A rocking motion and one foot swinging to and fro can herald a charge. The head is shaken with a loud slapping of the ears. An elephant charge is something you won't forget; I think Neil Murray, describes it best: 'The elephant often charges to the accompaniment of a blast of high-pitched trumpeting – caused by forcibly expelling air from its trunk – which sounds like an orchestra of outraged demons. Except perhaps for the prospect of imminent hanging, there can be few situations that concentrate the mind more wonderfully.'

The overwhelming desire to turn and flee is a natural reaction and must be weighed up with the certain fact that, should an elephant mean business, it can very easily outrun you. When infuriated, it normally attacks with the trunk held down and to the side or tucked under the chin. This is often followed by shrill screaming and sharp blasts. On occasions, no noise is made at all.

Movement is swift and one must react immediately. Little stops an elephant and, although it is an easy animal to hunt, it presents a difficult target head on, when charging and angry. Up steep slopes an elephant is somewhat slow, but remember that it is capable of pushing over trees with a circumference of 127 cm.

On trail one should always have an experienced tracker who will lead you out of such situations, leaving the trail leader to bring up the rear. Do not go after elephant unless you have a good tracker and definitely one who will not outrun all of you; the trail leader must have a sound knowledge of elephants.

Sound is a most important aspect in an elephant's daily life. When an elephant is frightened or nervous it produces high-pitched screams. I have witnessed this while observing elephant on open ground, where they feel quite vulnerable, or crossing a large, dry river. Young bulls are often noisy while on the move. They produce various other sounds including 'stomach rumblings', that are in fact produced by the vocal organs. These sounds are produced at will and they communicate them via the trunk or throat. Growling is an apt description of the sound. Elephants are highly social and sounds indicate a variety of signals, for example danger, fear and keeping in touch. Elephants use trunk and ear-spreading postures as expressive behaviour to convey anger, suspicion, threat or curiosity.

Elephants require vast quantities of food daily and wander great distances to satisfy their needs.

When disturbed they will, with one accord, remain perfectly still and silent. Many remain standing with whatever they have picked up or are holding in their mouths. With no sound the lead cow will move and the herd follows without hesitation. I would venture to suggest a telepathic system exists among elephants and that a silent (to human ears) language actually exists.

Elephants are extremely fond of bathing and wallowing in mud and water.

DIET

They spend between 16 and 18 hours per day eating and cover a considerable distance while feeding. They have a simple digestive system and require a large quantity of food – adult bulls eat between 180 kg and 270 kg of fodder per day.

Although elephants are essentially grass eaters – consuming up to 80 per cent of grass in their daily diet – they also eat a wide variety of vegetation such as leaves, mlala palm (*Hyphaene natalensis*), bark, roots, wild fruit of every description and seed pods of various Acacias, which they swallow whole; the thorns of the most formidable Acacia present no problem to them. When feeding on the mlala palm, this species can be approached quite easily due to the noise created as they tear out the fronds. These animals are adept at stripping bark from trees, destroying many trees in the process. Rocking of seed-bearing trees is a common activity and in doing this, they open up the soil and allow many seeds to enter the ground. Elephants are fond of crop raiding.

The animals move continuously while feeding and their tusks play a useful role in stripping and gouging bark, and in digging. The forelegs are also used for digging out roots, for scuffing bark and for digging shallow water holes.

The trunk, which is a highly sensitive organ, is the elephant's lifeline and is used for smelling, food gathering, drinking and as a weapon. Water is drawn up through the trunk and as much as 100 litres may be consumed at a time. They are dependent on water although they can go for a number of days without it. They cover great distances in their search for water and a great deal of habitat destruction is caused by injudicious placing of water holes, creating an unusually heavy impact on the surrounding vegetation. Elephants drink regularly and will go to great lengths to dig for water using both tusks and feet. The foot action is a series of kicks, with the trunk playing a part in drawing out mud or sand. The water percolates through, allowing the animal to drink after the mud has settled. They will often dig next to standing water which may be stagnant, in an attempt to find sweeter, fresher fluid. The holes thus made by the elephant provide water for a variety of antelope, warthog, baboons, birds and invertebrates. They are extremely fond of bathing and wallowing in water and mud.

Camps in private reserves are often the target for elephants since flowers are quite an attraction, coupled with a delight in breaking down and eating aloes, which in most cases, have been brought in by the owners. In the Kruger National Park, elephants have been observed browsing on no less than 70 different species of trees. The mopane tree (*Colophospermum mopane*) is one species of which elephant are particularly fond; the leaves are rich in protein and phosphorus.

FAECES

Fresh elephant dung is bright olive to yellow in colour. It has a strange, rather pleasant smell about it and stories of elephant hunters covering themselves in dung to disguise their scent are very often recounted. A good way of testing the freshness of dung, is to thrust your hand into the centre of it. If the dung is fresh, it will be warm inside. The colour changes as it dries, and a good tracker can tell when it was dropped by the elephant. When it is dark in colour it can be up to five or six hours old; thereafter it gradually lightens.

Stress factors cause a diarrhoeal action. When running, the faeces will often be spread out and not in the usual ball shape. Other factors that change the consistency include changes in vegetation and the seasons. For instance, during winter

The colour of elephant faeces is a good indication of how fresh or old it is.

there is a considerable reduction in the water content in plants and, consequently, there is as much as 40 per cent less water content in the faeces of most herbivores. Animals, therefore, become highly selective in their winter diet.

Dung beetles play a vital role in breaking up elephant dung. Certain species stick strictly to elephant faeces. Francolins scatter dung as they search for seeds.

An elephant's life span is governed by the life of its teeth. It will have six sets of molars which, when worn, are replaced and pushed out from behind. The tusks are modified upper incisors which grow out and upwards. The scientific name *Loxodonta* refers to the enamel pattern on the surface of the molars.

SPOOR

The forefoot is oval or circular with five toes.

The hind foot is cylindrical with four toes.

Forefoot
50–60 cm

Hind foot
60–65 cm

The spoor of an elephant is easily distinguished, the forefoot being larger than the hind foot and oval in shape. The hind foot is cylindrical and longer with four toes on each foot. The forefoot has five toes. Elephants, for all their size, walk in a narrow path with the hind foot coming up into the place of the forefoot or just behind it.

When tracking elephant in dust or on hard ground, stand back and gaze down the length of the stride. You will see the 'scuff' mark which characterizes the hind footprint. The forefoot is picked up, whereas the hind foot scrapes the ground. This is a good way of checking the direction in which a elephant is heading.

The sole of the foot is hard and like a mosaic pattern, with sharp pieces of hardened skin standing out. This enables the elephant to negotiate smooth surfaces easily. The action of movement is like a sponge, deadening the sound of leaves and branches underfoot. The soles of the feet contract when lifted and flatten as they are placed down. Elephants are most cautious in muddy and rocky conditions. Babies often fall flat onto their faces and slither about. They tend to avoid low-lying, muddy areas during heavy rain, preferring the high ground.

No gradient is too steep or surface too stony for an elephant. I have seen paths worn into sandstone where elephants have for years trekked up into the hills for water. In Kunene Province, Namibia, their paths are like worn vehicle tracks as they follow each other in single file out over the desert in search of water.

RUBBING

Elephants are fond of rubbing and will use convenient trees or rocks for this purpose. One finds evidence of this usually by observing mud which has been scraped off onto the trees. Elephants will dust themselves frequently after they have covered themselves in water and often when they are dry and hot. They do this by digging a hole in a favourite spot where the soil is soft. These holes are often found against a river bank.

An elephant stripping the bark of a tree.

Tree stumps or rocks are used for rubbing.

Tree Dassie
Dendrohyrax arboreus

Afrikaans: Boomdassie
Siswati: Imbila ye ma hlatsi

DESCRIPTION

OVERALL LENGTH: 50 cm   **MASS:** Up to 4,5 kg   **GESTATION:** About 210 days.
Tree dassies are nocturnal and arboreal, and are less gregarious than other dassie species. They occur on the eastern seaboard in coastal and sub-coastal forest, in Mpumalanga, the Natal Midlands and Swaziland. An isolated population is to be found in south-central Mozambique. Tree dassies live in rocky crevices and in the hollows of trees. Their cry is a piercing scream. They are dark brown in colour with long soft fur and a creamy-white dorsal spot.

DIET
Vegetarians; eat mostly leaves.

SPOOR
All dassies have similar spoor.

FAECES
Clustered. Defecate and urinate on the same spot.

Forefoot

0   5 cm

Hind foot

Actual size

R. Smithers

Tree dassies live in rocky crevices and in the hollows of trees.

Rock Dassie
Procavia capensis

Other English names: Rock rabbit or rock hyrax.
Afrikaans: Klipdassie   **Shona, Venda:** Mbila
Ndebele: Imbila   **Zulu, Xhosa, Siswati, Shangaan:** Mbili
Sotho, Tswana: Pela   **Nama/Damara:** !Âus

DESCRIPTION

OVERALL LENGTH: 50 cm   **MASS:** Up to 4,5 kg   **GESTATION:** 225 days.

Gregarious, these diurnal animals live in small or large colonies amongst koppies, hills and rocky outcrops. They have numerous enemies and rely on their senses of sight and sound to stay alive. They have an excellent ability to climb rocky slopes or trees. At the approach of danger they utter shrill barks and whistles and retreat with great haste to the safety of their rocky lairs. They are preyed upon by a variety of animals, the leopard and Verreaux's eagle *(Aquila verreauxii)* being high on the list. Pythons are also among their enemies. Dassie flesh has a pleasant flavour and sought after by various tribal Africans. They possess extremely long upper incisors which they use most effectively; they will bite anything that attempts to molest them. The rock dassie has a distinctive black dorsal spot.

DIET

Vegetarians; mainly leaves, grass, shoots, twigs and fruits.

FAECES

1 cm long. Dark in colour and strong-smelling due to urine; deposited in rock clefts and at the entrances to caves.

```
0                          5 cm
```

Rock dassies live amongst koppies, hills and rocky outcrops.

———————— **SPOOR** ————————
See yellow-spotted dassie (page 126) for
comparison and description.

Forefoot

Actual size

Hind foot

R. Smithers

Yellow-spotted Rock Dassie
Heterohyrax brucei

Afrikaans: Geelkoldassie
Shona: Mbira **Ndebele:** Imbila

DESCRIPTION

OVERALL LENGTH: 45–55 cm MASS: 2,5–3,5 kg

The habitat of this dassie is similar to that of the rock dassie, but with a far more restricted range. It does not occur in South Africa, except in the Northern Province. The distinguishing feature is the yellow spot situated on the back (mid-dorsally). Yellow-spotted dassies are smaller than rock dassies.

DIET

Vegetarian; leaves, grass, shoots, twigs, fruits and bulbs.

FAECES

Deposited in selected latrines which are often piled fairly high. They urinate in other spots, mainly on sloping rock. Because of its crystallizing action, the urine is prized in South Africa for its medicinal properties. This accounts for the slabs found on rock surfaces which have been urinated on. The urine has a strong, musky odour.

0   5 cm

The distinguishing feature of this dassie is the yellow spot on its back.

The toes have small blunt nails instead of claws. The second toe has a nail for grooming. The soles are naked and moistened by a gland. They are so designed as to act as a suction pad, enabling these animals to run up near-vertical faces. There are four toes on the front feet, and three on the hind.

Forefoot

Actual size

Hind foot

R. Smithers

Black Rhinoceros

Diceros bicornis

Afrikaans: Swartrenoster **Zulu, Sindebele:** uBhejane
Transvaal Sotho, Tswana: Tshukudu **Xhosa:** Umkhombe
Venda: Thema **Herero:** Ngara **Tsonga:** Mhelembe
Kung Bushman: Khi **Shona:** Chipenbere, Nhema
Lozi: Sukulu **Yei:** Unshunguzu **Nama/Damara:** !Nabas

DESCRIPTION

SHOULDER HEIGHT: 1,6 m **MASS:** 900–1 000 kg
GESTATION: 15–16 months; single calf **SPEED:** Maximum of 45 km/h.

The hook-lipped, or black, rhinoceros has a distinctive prehensile lip. It holds its head high and is smaller than the square-lipped, or white, rhinoceros. The alternate name, black rhinoceros, alludes to it being darker in colour than the white rhinoceros. An agile animal, the hook-lipped rhinoceros can display considerable aggression when alarmed. It is normally shy and usually solitary. Its eyesight is poor but it possesses exceptional hearing and a good sense of smell. The head is held horizontal in a charge – the whole front portion of the body lifts off the ground when it tosses its target. The tail is held erect on the run. The black rhinoceros has a wide vocal range and, I believe, can communicate at a level inaudible to human hearing. Breathing is also an important part of communication. A sharp, strong snort followed by a fluttering sound is an alarm or warning sound; a hoarse sound is used to make contact with another rhinoceros. It also makes loud puffing and snorting sounds. The calf runs behind the mother.

DIET

Browser, also known to graze seasonally. Usually found in thickets where it eats shrubs, twigs and leaves. Thorns present no problem.

FAECES

Usually defecates in middens or along various routes; dung is scattered with the hind legs. Easily identified by its fibrous and woody nature. Different colour to the dung of the white rhinoceros.

Faeces contain wood chips.

Endangered species

A black rhinoceros on the alert.

SPOOR

Much more compact and smaller than that of the square-lipped rhinoceros (page 130). Urinates backwards against vegetation and then kicks back, often breaking up the vegetation. This action is a form of marking territory and communication.

Spoor is circular and compact.

20–25 cm

White Rhinoceros
Ceratotherium simum

Afrikaans: Witrenoster   **Zulu, Siswati:** uMkhombe
Tswana: Tshukudu, Mogohu, Kgetlwa
Transvaal Sotho: Tshukudu, Mogohu   **Venda:** Tshugulu
Sindebele: Umhofu   **Shona:** Chipembere

DESCRIPTION

SHOULDER HEIGHT: 1,8 m   **MASS:** Up to 2 000 kg
GESTATION: 18 months; single calf at intervals of 3 years.

The jaw is square and the head is carried low. Larger than the black rhinoceros, it is by contrast, far more placid and less prone to attack. Curious by nature, tapping sounds draw its attention. In the event of a fast approach, get behind a tree. Eyesight is poor, but both hearing and smell are acute. The tail loops over the back when the animal is on the move. It can reach speeds of up to 40 km/h over short distances. It is fond of mud wallows and rubbing posts which are often polished to a fine surface. The calf walks in front of the mother.

DIET
They are grass eaters.

FAECES

Deposits its dung in large middens. Droppings are large and darkish-green when fresh, turning black with age. Resembles elephant dung in composition. Territorial bulls urinate backwards in a fine controlled spray. Trees and bushes are marked using the horn.

A smoothly polished rubbing post.

The calf generally precedes the mother.

─────────────────── **S P O O R** ───────────────────
Three-toed; forefoot is 28 cm long and 24 cm wide. Well-used trails are often formed. They are experts at negotiating steep slopes. Spoor is longer than that of the hook-lipped rhinoceros.

The spoor is longer than that of the black rhinoceros.

20–28 cm

Burchell's Zebra

Equus burchellii

Afrikaans: Bontsebra **Zulu, Xhose:** Dube **Ndebele:** Idube
Shona: Mbizi **Shangaan:** Tsonga, Mangwe
Sotho, Tswana: Pitse ya naga **Siswati:** Lidvubu **Lozi:** Pizi
Yei: Umbiyi **Nama/Damara:** !Goreb, !Goareb

DESCRIPTION

SHOULDER HEIGHT: 1,3 m **MASS:** 227–325 kg
GESTATION: 365 days; single young. Breed throughout the year.

Zebras possess good eyesight. Highly sociable animals, they congregate in herds from five to 30 in number and are often associated with blue wildebeest. They produce a high-pitched bark, neigh and squeal. This species is frequently preyed upon by lion. Zebras are water dependent, they will travel many kilometres to find water and, when necessary, will dig for it.

DIET

Grazes, but will occasionally browse. They dig for rhizomes or roots.

FAECES

Not unlike warthog droppings on first appearance. Closer examination will reveal cracks across the centre and a more elongated shape.

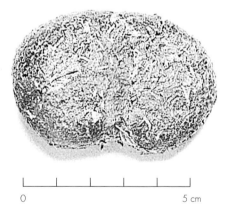

L___I___I___I___I___I
0   5 cm

Although they may occasionally browse, zebras are essentially grazers.

SPOOR

Distinctively shaped like a horse with a single, enlarged toe. Like the horse, it possesses great speed. Tip of the hoof is dug into the soil when running. Poachers will sometimes walk donkeys over zebra spoor to confuse any followers.

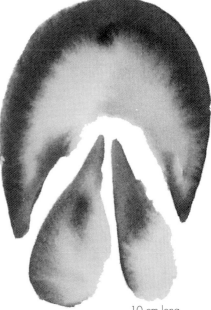

10 cm long

Mountain Zebra

Equus zebra zebra

Two subspecies are recognized: Cape & Hartmann's
Afrikaans: (Kaapse of Hartmanse) Bergsebra   Xhosa: Dauwa
Cape Hottentot: Daou   Bushman: Dou
(Hartmann's) Herero: Ngorlo, Hambarundu
Nama/Damara: !Hom !goreb

DESCRIPTION

SHOULDER HEIGHT: 1,2–1,4 m   MASS: 227–272 kg   GESTATION: 365 days.

The agile mountain zebra lives in arid, stony regions. The Cape mountain zebra is confined to the southern mountains of the Cape. Its black stripes are broader than those of Hartmann's mountain zebra, which occurs in the mountainous parts of Namibia and southern Angola. Hartmann's mountain zebra has a well-developed mane, whereas the Cape mountain zebra has a short mane. Both subspecies have a well-defined dewlap below the throat. Hartmann's mountain zebra will range well into the desert in search of new growth.

The mountain zebra is capable of going without water for up to three days. When in search of water it will dig down to 1 metre. Unlike Burchell's zebra, its call is a low, plaintive neigh.

DIET

Grazer. Feeds on tufted grasses.

FAECES

Similar to Burchell's zebra with cracks across the centre.

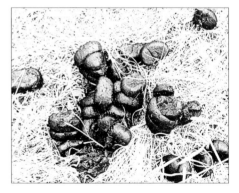

Endangered: Cape mountain zebra

The agile mountain zebra lives in arid, stony regions.

―――――― **S P O O R** ――――――
Narrower and somewhat smaller than
Burchell's zebra, with sharper indentation. Mountain zebra follow well-defined
trails across mountains and gravel flats.

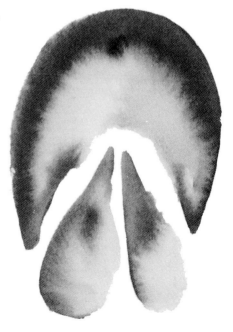

10 cm

Bushpig

Potamochoerus porcus

Afrikaans: Bosvark **Xhosa, Zulu:** Ngulube
Shangaan: Khumba, Ngulube M'hlati **Ndebele:** Ngulugunda
Sotho: Kolobe, Sodi, Ya-thab Kolobe, Moru **Venda:** Nguluvhe
Tswana: Kolobe ya naga **Shona:** Humba, Nguruve
Siswati: Ingulnbe ye siganga **Tswana:** Kolobe ya naga
Lozi: Ngili **Yei:** Unkutula **Nama/Damara:** !Garohagub

DESCRIPTION

SHOULDER HEIGHT: 65–75 cm **MASS:** 70–80 kg **GESTATION:** 120 days; 3–7 piglets.
Mainly nocturnal, the bushpig is a gregarious but tough, no nonsense animal. It lives
in large sounders of up to 10 or more individuals. It is a dangerous adversary with
extremely sharp tusks and should be given a wide berth. The tail is held down when
running as opposed to the warthog, which holds its tail vertically. It is a good swimmer. The voice consists of soft grunting. It is preyed on by leopard and lion.
Numbers have increased in areas where carnivore numbers have decreased.

DIET

Roots, bulbs, seeds, fruit, grasses, carrion, reptiles, insects and birds' eggs.
Also raids crops. Will chew old bones.

FAECES

Being omnivorous, faeces contain the
remains of various organic substances
and turn dark with age.

0   5 cm

A bushpig forages for roots and bulbs.

SPOOR

About the same length as that of the warthog, but more circular.

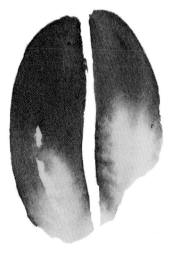

Actual size

Warthog
Phacochoerus aethiopicus

Afrikaans: Vlakvark **Zulu:** Ndlovudalana, Ndhlovudawana
Shangaan, Tsonga: Ngulube **Lozi, Tswana, Sotho:** Kolobe
Venda: Phangwa **Herero:** Mbinda **Ndebele:** Ngulube
Shona: Njiri **Siswati:** Budzayikatana **Yei:** Ungili
Nama/Damara: Dirib, gairib

DESCRIPTION

SHOULDER HEIGHT: 72 cm **MASS:** 68–72 kg
GESTATION: 160–170 days; average litter 3–4 piglets.

The warthog is a gregarious, diurnal animal that lives in abandoned aardvark holes. It enters its hole backwards, a protective measure which enables it to make a quick escape. The male has two pairs of warts. The pair on the muzzle is absent in the female. The warthog is fond of wallowing and rubbing its mud-covered body on stumps, rocks and trunks of trees. Its habit of rooting for grass rhizomes often leads to the creation of a wallow. Sight is poor although it has good scent and hearing. When approached a warthog will often advance towards you, running off only when certain what you are. It falls prey to lion, leopard, wild dog and cheetah.

DIET

Grass, roots, bulbs and tubers. Will eat fruit, although it favours short grass. It feeds by resting on its front knees. Requires water daily.

FAECES

Round in shape and dull, greenish brown in colour. Not unlike zebra faeces which are more elongated and crack across the middle.

Anthills make convenient rubbing spots.

```
0                    5 cm
```

The gregarious warthog lives in abandoned aardvark holes.

————— S P O O R —————

Four toes on each foot. The lateral toes, as with the bushpig, do not touch the ground as they are located higher up on the leg. Length of spoor is similar to bushpig, but width is narrower and spoor is more pointed in the front.

Actual size

Hippopotamus
Hippopotamus amphibius

Afrikaans: Seekoei **Xhosa, Zulu, Siswati:** Mvubu
Shangaan, Tsonga: Mpfubu **Tswana, Sotho:** Kubu
Venda: Mvuvu **Shona:** Mvuu, Ngwindi **Ndebele:** Imvubu
Lozi: Kubu **Yei:** Unvuva **Nama/Damara:** !Khaos

DESCRIPTION

SHOULDER HEIGHT: 1,4 m **MASS:** 1 700–2 000 kg **GESTATION:** About 250 days.
Mating takes place in the water. The young are either born on land or in the water, but are suckled underwater.

It is extreme folly to move between water and a grazing hippopotamus. Old bulls and cows can be dangerous and usually adopt a truculent attitude towards anyone who comes close. Many a boat has felt the brunt of venturing too near, some even to a point of having been bitten in half. Besides being a good swimmer, a hippopotamus can run underwater (as fast as a man can walk), on the bottom of the river bed; a hippopotamus can remain underwater for up to six minutes. In a mock charge this mammal moves in a lunging fashion above the water, but in a real attack it remains just below the surface.

Mainly nocturnal, it moves some distance when feeding, uttering grunts, and will make for water with great speed when disturbed. Loud bellows erupt when fighting. The hippopotamus is nature's natural dredge, displacing silt and sand near banks and thus allowing a continual flow of water.

FAECES

The dung is not unlike that of an elephant that has fed on grass. On land it scatters its dung, usually against a bush, with a sideways wagging of the tail. Defecation also occurs in water where it is fed upon by fish for its nutrients.

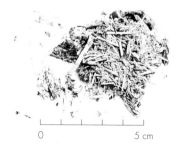

0　　　　　5 cm

DIET

A grazer, it has a non-ruminating, three-chambered stomach. Eats up to 130 kg of grass in a night.

The spoor shows four distinctly splayed toes.

Old bulls and cows usually adopt a truculent attitude towards anyone who comes close.

SPOOR

Four toes. All four, both lateral and middle, are equally developed in length. Well-worn paths, some 20 cm wide, lead up from rivers, the four-toed tracks running parallel, and clearly indicating a 'middelmannetjie'. Channels also lead out of marginal swamps, providing protection for fish and opening up vegetation.

25 cm

Giraffe
Giraffa camelopardalis

Afrikaans: Kameelperd **Zulu:** Ndhlulamithi
Shangaan: Nthutlwa **Tswana:** Thutlwa **Sotho:** Thutlwa,
Thitlwa **Venda:** Thuda **Ndebele:** Htundla, Ndlulamithi
Siswati: Indlulamitsi **Lozi:** Tutwa **Yei:** Unveweshe
Nama/Damara: !Garo!naib

DESCRIPTION

SHOULDER HEIGHT: 5–6 m **MASS:** Up to 1 270 kg
GESTATION: 15 months; single calf, occasionally twins; breeds year round.
Both sexes have horns. The cow's horns turn inwards and are well tufted. It is a gregarious animal with a keen sense of smell and good hearing and sight. It is capable of moving at speeds of up to 50 km/h. It feeds during the day and at night. The giraffe is preyed upon by lion despite the fact that it is capable of delivering a fearful kick which could easily kill a lion. In spite of being extremely long, there are only seven vertebrae in a giraffe's neck – as found in other mammals. It is a silent animal, occasionally uttering grunts and moans.

DIET

A browser, known to graze seasonally in some areas. Not dependent on water; stays for long periods in waterless areas.

SPOOR

Unmistakable, square-toed print. The giraffe is prone to breaking its limbs, caused by slipping on wet surfaces.

FAECES

Pellet-shaped (longer in bulls than in cows), causing confusion at times with kudu faeces. Pellets are flattened at one end and tend to be more scattered than kudu pellets because of the drop.

0   5 cm

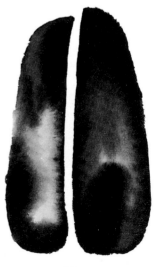

19 cm

The cow's horns turn inwards and are well tufted.

Damara Dik-dik

Madoqua kirkii

Afrikaans: Damara Dik-dik
Herero: Thini (Shortridge)
Ovambo: Tingu (Shortridge) **Nama/Damara:** | Hauib

DESCRIPTION

SHOULDER HEIGHT: 35–40 cm   **MASS:** 3–5 kg   **GESTATION:** 170 days.
The Damara dik-dik inhabits bush and scrub thickly strewn with rock. This species can be found in Damaraland, Kunene Province and Etosha in Namibia, and also in southern Angola. Its range extends beyond southern Africa. A shy, diminutive animal, it is usually found in pairs. It marks its territory with secretions from preorbital glands. The female has no horns.

DIET

Browser. Appears to be independent of water. Will utilize leaves and flowers.

FAECES

Faeces have a distinctive point and are 0,5–1 cm long. Communal dung middens (within home range) are established, which can cover an area of up to 4 metres by 5 metres. Scrape marks are a feature of these middens. (Information supplied by Sharon Montgomery, Namibia.)

A female Damara dik-dik.

─────────────── **S P O O R** ───────────────

A neat, pointed track about half the length of a matchbox; 2,5 cm long.

Actual size

145

Oribi
Ourebia ourebi

Afrikaans: Oorbietjie
Zulu, Xhosa, Siswati: Wula, Iwula
Tswana: Phuduhudu kgamane **Lozi:** Kamunda **Yei:** Untungu

DESCRIPTION

SHOULDER HEIGHT: 51–66 cm (on average)
MASS: 14–20 kg **GESTATION:** About 210 days.

A swift, inquisitive antelope that lies up in tall grass and is mainly found in grassland savanna. It has a peculiar gait and when alarmed, utters a sharp whistle. The oribi is distributed throughout the Eastern Cape Province, KwaZulu-Natal, southeastern Mpumalanga, Mozambique and southeastern Zimbabwe, and is usually found in pairs or small groups. This species is easily recognized by its short, white, bushy tail visible when seen running off.

DIET

A grazer; dependent on water. Prefers short grass.

FAECES

Often found in middens. Not unlike that of the grey duiker.

0   5 cm

Oribi are found mostly in grassland savanna.

--------------- **SPOOR** ---------------
Pointed and fairly broad at the base.
3,5 cm long.

Actual size

Suni
Neotragus moschatus

Other English name: Livingstone's Antelope
Afrikaans: Soenie **Zulu:** Nhlengane

DESCRIPTION

SHOULDER HEIGHT: 35–40 cm **MASS:** 5,5–9 kg **GESTATION:** Little is known.
A small, shy, secretive animal inhabiting thick, dense bush and found solitarily or in pairs. A musky scent is excreted from facial glands and its territories are marked with deposits from these glands. Swift and not easily observed, this species has been seen in the Sihangwane forest in northern Tongaland. This species is found in Zululand and northwards into Mozambique. Besides the blue duiker, it is the smallest antelope in southern Africa.

DIET

Browser; very selective. Leaves, shoots, fruit, twigs and shrubs. Independent of water like the steenbok. It feeds in the early morning and late evening.

FAECES

Smallest of all the antelope.

0   5 cm

This shy animal is found solitarily or in pairs.

——————— S P O O R ———————

Similar to that of the red duiker although it is more pointed. 3 cm long.

Actual size

Grysbok
Raphicerus melanotis

Afrikaans: Grysbok
Xhosa: Ngxungxu
Southern Sotho: Phuti

DESCRIPTION

SHOULDER HEIGHT: 54 cm   **MASS:** 10–12 kg   **GESTATION:** 185 days.
Grysbok are found in the Addo and Mountain Zebra national parks, along the eastern coastal belt of South Africa as well as in the southeastern Cape, westwards to the Cape Peninsula. During the mating season they occur in pairs, but at other times are solitary. They are larger and stouter than Sharpe's grysbok and have long ears. They lie flat when threatened and prefer open grass areas, often in close proximity to the base of hills. They are mainly nocturnal and lie up in tall grass during the day.

DIET

They graze and browse and can go without water for long periods.

FAECES

More rounded and flattened at ends.

0   5 cm

SPOOR

A neat, pointed track.

The grysbok has short horns.

Actual size

Sharpe's Grysbok

Raphicerus sharpei

Afrikaans: Sharpe se Grysbok
Shona: Himba **Ndebele:** Isanempa
Shangaan: Pitsipitsi **Siswati:** Mawumbane

DESCRIPTION

SHOULDER HEIGHT: 40 cm **MASS:** 9 kg **GESTATION:** 165 days; single young. Can be confused with the steenbok which is slightly taller. When alarmed it runs away with its head held low whereas the steenbok carries its head high. It is found in pairs or singly over a wide area of the eastern escarpment, south to Swaziland and north to Zimbabwe. It has been recorded in the Waterberg Mountains of the Northern Province. When pursued, it hides in disused aardvark holes.

DIET

Browser, occasionally also feeding on young grass.

FAECES

Deposit their droppings in middens in neat piles.

```
L___I___I___I___I___I
0                5 cm
```

SPOOR

Identical to the steenbok.

Actual size

Sharpe's grysbok are found in pairs or singly.

151

Grey Rhebok
Pelea capreolus

Afrikaans: Vaalribbok
Xhosa, Zulu, Siswati: Liza
Tswana: Lehele   **Sotho:** Letsa

DESCRIPTION

SHOULDER HEIGHT: 70–76 cm   **MASS:** 18–23 kg   **GESTATION:** 260 days.
This species occurs on flat-topped, grass-covered mountains, in groups of up to 20; old males live singly. The grey rhebok occurs throughout the Cape, Lesotho, KwaZulu-Natal, eastern Free State, Swaziland and southeastern Mpumalanga. They are not found in the Kruger National Park, but are endemic to southern Africa. They have good sight, hearing and sense of smell. The voice has been described as a sharp cough. These animals show a distinctive white tail when running off.

DIET
It is exclusively a grazer.

FAECES
Not collected.

SPOOR
Not collected.

The male grey rhebok carries upright horns.

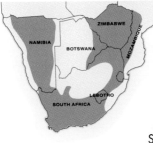

Klipspringer
Oreotragus oreotragus

Afrikaans: Klipspringer **Shona:** Ngururu **Ndebele:** Igogo
Sotho: Kome **Tswana:** Kololo **Shangaan, Venda:** Ngululu
Siswati: Ligoka **Nama/Damara:** ‖ Khâises

DESCRIPTION

SHOULDER HEIGHT: 50–61 cm **MASS:** 15 kg **GESTATION:** About 210 days.

A compact, inquisitive animal that blends in well with its surroundings. It is widely distributed, frequenting koppies and hilly, rocky countryside. Where suitable habitat occurs, it has definite home ranges. This species is a phenomenal jumper; it is able to go up vertical faces, balancing expertly on its cylindrical hooves. The klipspringer makes a short snorting sound.

DIET

Principally a browser. Independent of water, but drinks water when available.

FAECES

Up to 1,3 cm long; rounded and pointed.

SPOOR

The track is unlike that of any other antelope, each slot consisting of two small oval pits, close together, not unlike the imprints of the tips of two fingers.

```
0                    5 cm
```

Actual size

The klipspringer is at home in hilly country.

153

Blue Duiker
Philantomba monticola

Afrikaans: Blouduiker **Zulu:** Iphiti
Nama/Damara: Dôas, |Nâus
Tswana: Phuti

DESCRIPTION

SHOULDER HEIGHT: 30–35 cm **MASS:** 4–6 kg **GESTATION:** About 165 days.
This is the smallest antelope in southern Africa. It is a shy creature, well-adapted to living in forests, and inhabits thick forest and bush from the Eastern Cape Province, KwaZulu-Natal, Swaziland into Mozambique and eastern Zimbabwe. It drinks regularly. Being nocturnal, it lies up during the day. It marks its territories with secretions from the facial glands. This duiker is preyed upon by crowned eagles and pythons, and is also heavily poached.

DIET
A browser taking leaves and fruit.

FAECES
Round pellets with pointed tips.

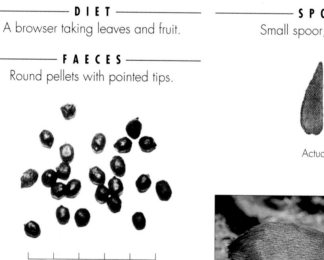

0   5 cm

SPOOR
Small spoor, 2 cm long.

Actual size

The smallest antelope in southern Africa.

Red Duiker
Cephalophus natalensis

Afrikaans: Rooiduiker
Zulu: Umsumpe **Venda:** Phithi
Siswati: Umsumbi

DESCRIPTION

SHOULDER HEIGHT: 41–46 cm **MASS:** 13 kg **GESTATION:** Unknown.

This compact, small antelope inhabits dense, well-forested areas of KwaZulu-Natal through the former Zululand and Mozambique. Mainly nocturnal, it is secretive and shy and found, as a rule, singly. Little is known about this species.

DIET

A browser, it eats fruits, leaves and shoots and is water dependent.

FAECES

1–2 cm long; fairly pointed.

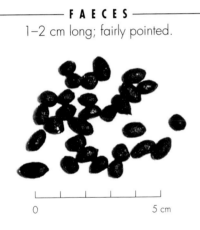

0   5 cm

SPOOR

Similar in shape to that of the blue duiker, but slightly longer and more pointed.

Actual size

The red duiker is dependent on water.

Common Duiker

Sylvicapra grimmia

Afrikaans: Duiker **Tswana:** Phuṯi **Shona:** Mhembwe
Ndebele: Impunzi **Sotho:** Phuthi **Venda:** Nfsa
Xhosa, Zulu, Siswati: Mpunzi **Shangaan:** Mhuti
Lozi: Puti **Yei:** Unsa **Nama/Damara:** Dôas

DESCRIPTION

SHOULDER HEIGHT: 60 cm **MASS:** 12–16 kg **GESTATION:** 210 days.

This is a common species found throughout southern Africa. Mainly nocturnal, although often seen in daylight, this elusive, shy animal keeps to thick bush during the heat of the day. It is found singly or in pairs. The largest of our three duikers, it is independent of water. The name 'duiker' is derived from the Afrikaans word meaning diver, and describes the characteristic diving action of the animal when fleeing.

DIET

Mainly a browser, the common duiker includes fruits, leaves, grass and roots in its diet. This species is fond of feeding in cultivated land.

FAECES

Round with tiny, pointed end. Found in neat piles in a fixed area.

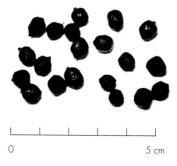

0   5 cm

The shy, elusive common duiker.

Narrow, pointed track; 3,5 cm long.

Actual size

Steenbok

Raphicerus campestris

Afrikaans: Steenbok **Tswana:** Phuduhudu **Shona:** Mhene
Ndebele: Ingina **Xhosa:** Shabanga **Zulu:** Qhina
Venda: Phuluvhulu **Shangaan:** Shipene **Sotho:** Thiane
Siswati: Lingcina **Lozi:** Kabu **Yei:** Ughwi
Nama/Damara: !Aris, !Airis

DESCRIPTION

SHOULDER HEIGHT: 50–56 cm **MASS:** 12–14 kg
GESTATION: Approximately 165 days; single young.

Found throughout southern Africa in arid and temperate regions, in vleis, open bush and woodland. It is a swift animal that zigzags as it runs, often stopping a short way off to look back. The ears are large and distinctive. Diurnal and nocturnal, it is fond of lying up in tall grass or under low bushes. It is found in pairs during the breeding season; otherwise it is found singly.

DIET

Browser, entirely independent of water.

FAECES

Narrow and pointed.

SPOOR

Broader than the suni. Distinctly pointed. 3 cm long.

Actual size

0   5 cm

The steenbok has distinctive, large ears.

Blesbok
Damaliscus dorcas phillipsi

Afrikaans: Blesbok
Tswana, Transvaal Sotho: Nonê, Nônô

DESCRIPTION

SHOULDER HEIGHT: 93 cm   **MASS:** 59–80 kg   **GESTATION:** 240 days.
The blesbok, like the bontebok, is a subspecies of *Damaliscus dorcas*. It is found on the Highveld where it is capable of withstanding extreme cold. Duller than the bontebok, it is, however, similar in physical structure. The facial markings of the two subspecies are conspicuously different (see page 162) and help to distinguish the two. Both sexes have horns. Found in herds, this species is highly territorial; if disturbed the blesbok runs upwind in single file.

DIET

Purely a grazer; drinks regularly.

FAECES

Almost identical in shape to that of the bontebok.

Blesbok midden

0   5 cm

Blesbok are found in herds and are highly territorial.

SPOOR

Similar to that of the bontebok, but shorter in length.

Bontebok

Blesbok

Forefoot
Actual size

Bontebok
Damaliscus dorcas dorcas

Afrikaans: Bontebok

DESCRIPTION

SHOULDER HEIGHT: 83–99 cm **MASS:** 59–95 kg **GESTATION:** 240 days.

The bontebok and the smaller blesbok are distinct subspecies of *Damaliscus dorcas*. Both sexes carry horns but those of the ewe are more slender than those of the ram. The bontebok was brought perilously close to extinction, but is now protected in private and state reserves. The ram which is territorial remains in its home ranges throughout the year. The bontebok has a limited geographical range; it is confined to the southwestern Cape. This species is striking in appearance, showing a distinctive blaze on the face.

DIET
Purely a grazer.

FAECES
Same as that of the blesbok.

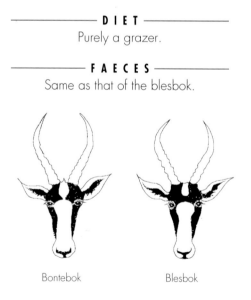

Bontebok   Blesbok

0   5 cm

Bontebok can be distinguished from the similar Blesbok by their facial markings.

SPOOR

Slightly larger than the blesbok.

Forefoot
6,5 cm

Hind foot
6 cm

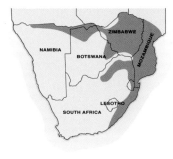

Reedbuck
Redunca arundinum

Other English name: Southern Reedbuck
Afrikaans: Rietbok **Xhosa:** Ntlangu **Zulu:** Nxala
Shangaan: Nhlangu **Sotho:** Lekwena **Venda:** Dahvu
Shona: Bimha **Ndebele:** Umziki **Tswana:** Sebugatla
Siswati: Inhlangu **Lozi:** Mutobo **Yei:** Unvwi
Damara/Nama: ǂĀ!aris

DESCRIPTION

SHOULDER HEIGHT: 85 cm **MASS:** 65–68 kg **GESTATION:** About 210 days.
Reedbuck generally inhabit areas of grassland and floodplains, favouring reedbeds alongside permanent water. A shrill whistle, often heard at night, is uttered when alarmed. They are preyed upon by lion, wild dogs, hyaena, leopard and cheetah. On occasion they will lie flat when suspicious. They run with a rocking motion and frequently stop and look back to the disturbance. The tail is conspicuous when running. They feed during early morning and late evening, lying up in tall grass during the day. In the Okavango they favour small islands in the *melapo* or lagoons. They occur singly, in pairs and in small groups of five or six. Only the males have horns. Reedbuck populations are declining in much of their range due to human predation.

DIET
Entirely grazers. Water dependent.

FAECES
Small pellets in clusters.

0   5 cm

Only the male reedbuck carries the forward-curved and partially ridged horns.

SPOOR

Not unlike that of the impala; more splayed out. About 6 cm long.

Actual size

Mountain Reedbuck
Redunca fulvorufula

Afrikaans: Rooiribbok **Sotho:** Letlabo **Venda:** Davhu
Tswana: Lehele **Siswati:** Shitswiyo **Xhosa, Zulu:** Nxala

DESCRIPTION

SHOULDER HEIGHT: 63–76 cm **MASS:** 22–27 kg **GESTATION:** 210 days.

The mountain reedbuck is more gregarious than the reedbuck. It lives in mountainous terrain, using rocks and boulders as cover. In the heat of the day it rests, coming down to drink and feed in the cool of the evening.

DIET

Predominantly grass, but will also feed on broad leaves and small twigs.

FAECES

Rounder and smaller than the reedbuck.

0   5 cm

As the name suggests, this reedbuck lives in mountainous terrain.

Slightly more splayed than that of the reedbuck. 5 cm long.

Actual size

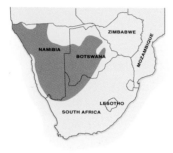

Springbok
Antidorcas marsupialis

Afrikaans: Springbok **Herero:** Menyeh
Tswana: Tshephe, Maponye **Sotho:** Tshephe
Nama/Damara: | Gûb

--- **DESCRIPTION** ---

SHOULDER HEIGHT: 78–84 cm **MASS:** 36–50 kg **GESTATION:** 160 days.
This is the only gazelle found south of the Zambezi. Both sexes have horns which are lyre-shaped and heavily ridged; the males' horns are heavier and longer than those of the females. Springbok live in habitats ranging from dry areas of the Kalahari to the barren regions of the Namib. They have good eyesight and are highly gregarious. When moving at speed, they will bound into the air with a stiff-legged 'pronking' action, during which the hooves are bunched.

--- **DIET** ---

Both browses and grazes. Roots, bulbs, short grass and leaves of various bushes are taken. Independent of water but will drink regularly when water is available.

--- **FAECES** ---

Clusters and single pellets.

--- **SPOOR** ---

Similar to the impala; 5 cm long.

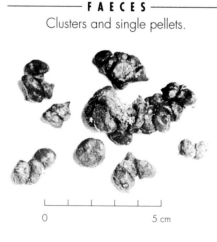

0   5 cm

Actual size

Springbok have heavily ringed, lyre-shaped horns.

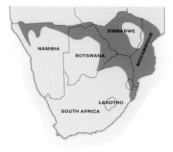

Impala
Aepyceros melampus

Afrikaans: Rooibok **Zulu, Siswati, Ndebele:** Mpala
Shangaan: Mhala **Tswana, Sotho, Venda:** Phala
Shona: Mhara **Lozi:** Pala **Yei:** Umpala
Nama/Damara: Arab

DESCRIPTION

SHOULDER HEIGHT: 91 cm **MASS:** 45–55 kg **GESTATION:** 180–210 days.
They have acute hearing and have been known to frighten elephants by uttering loud snorts when alarmed by the approach of humans. They fight a great deal during the mating season, uttering long, drawn out snorts, and are quite capable of killing one another at such times. This preoccupation affects their vigilance and it is often possible to pass close by a herd without disturbing them. They remain persistently in overgrazed areas. Impalas are excellent jumpers. They can often be seen in the company of baboons, and are preyed upon by lion, cheetah, leopard and, to a great extent, the Cape hunting dog. In overcast, windy weather they often lie down. The black tufts above the hooves on the hind legs conceal scent glands.

DIET
Both browsers and grazers. They utilise a wide variety of plants and drink regularly.

FAECES
Both pellets and clustered faeces are found. Herds and bachelor groups deposit faeces in middens. Middens are often found next to game trails and in open areas.

0   5 cm

A common widespread antelope of the savanna region.

SPOOR

Sharp, neat and pointed hooves. Follow well-worn trails to water. 4–6 cm long.

Actual size

Blue Wildebeest

Connochaetes taurinus

Afrikaans: Blouwildebees **Ndebele, Zulu, Xhosa:** Nkhonhoni
Shona, Siswati: Ngongoni **Sotho, Tswana:** Kgokong
Lozi: Kokoñu **Yei:** Unzonzo **Nama/Damara:** Gaob
Venda: Khongoini **Shangaan:** Hongonyi

DESCRIPTION

SHOULDER HEIGHT: 1,27–1,30 m **MASS:** 185–249 kg **GESTATION:** 224–250 days.
These are gregarious animals. The bulls are highly territorial and stake out specific areas; the square-lipped (white) rhinoceros displays similar behaviour. They create numerous rolling grounds, usually in open areas that provide good visibility, and often deposit their dung here. They are fond of rubbing the boss and horns on trees within their territories. Their scent forms an important part of communication. Although they are swift runners, they nevertheless fall prey to lions. The voice is an abrupt, loud snort and they communicate with a loud, nasal 'kwang' sound. They often associate with zebra and, although their sight is not as good as a zebra's, they have keen hearing and sense of smell.

DIET

Grazers. Require water daily.

FAECES

Pellets are both single and clustered. They roll in their own dung.

0   5 cm

Blue wildebeest have an overall dark grey colour with a bluish sheen.

Broader than that of the red hartebeest. 11–13 cm long.

11–13 cm

Black Wildebeest

Connochaetes gnou

Afrikaans: Swartwildebees
Hottentot: Gnu

DESCRIPTION

SHOULDER HEIGHT: 1,14 m **MASS:** 113–159 kg **GESTATION:** 224–240 days.

The Hottentot (Khoi) name, *Gnu*, is derived from the word referring to the sound this animal makes – a metallic, ringing, snort. The black wildebeest maintains territories and, during the rut, will endeavour to herd as many cows into their area as possible. Bachelor groups consist of bulls of varying ages. Cows and calves wander over territories freely. Both sexes have horns. Stocky, swift cantering, with the head held erect, is characteristic. Distribution in former times extended into the KwaZulu-Natal Drakensberg and Cape, but today it is confined mainly to the Free State.

DIET

Grazer. Will also feed on succulents and shrubs. Drinking water essential.

FAECES

Similar to that of blue wildebeest; found in single pellets and clusters. Bulls maintain their territories fiercely and mark them with pedal glands, faeces and urine.

The black wildebeest has a stocky, swift cantering gait.

SPOOR

Spoor is smaller than that of the blue wildebeest. 9 cm long.

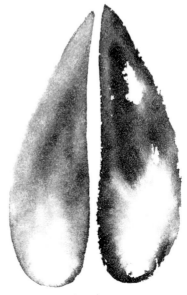

Actual size

Tsessebe
Damaliscus lunatus

Afrikaans: Basterhartbees **Shangaan:** Nondo
Tswana: Tshesebe **Sotho:** Tshentshebe **Ndebele:** Inkolomi
Shono: Nondo **Siswati:** Mzansi **Lozi:** Sebesebe
Yei: Unsuru **Nama/Damara:** ‖ Khamab

DESCRIPTION

SHOULDER HEIGHT: 1,2 m **MASS:** 136–145 kg **GESTATION:** 240 days; single young.
The tsessebe, with its well-developed shoulders, is the swiftest antelope in southern Africa. Both the sexes have horns. This antelope appears to have favoured stamping grounds and rubbing on old stumps is known to occur. Bulls maintain well-patrolled territories. The cows and calves live permanently within these areas from which all intruder bulls are ejected.

It stands on anthills in order to obtain a better view. Inquisitive creatures with good eyesight, they will often trot towards you. They are associated with zebra and wildebeest. A change in habitat has, without doubt, contributed to their decline. Formerly a rare species in the Northern Province and Mpumalanga, they are now found in increasing numbers, especially in private reserves, and in the northern parts of the Kruger National Park, Mozambique, Caprivi, and the Okavango north to Chobe and Zimbabwe. The young are preyed upon by all the large carnivores.

DIET

Entirely grazers.

FAECES

More pointed than that of the roan or sable antelopes.

```
0                              5 cm
```

Tsessebe have well-developed shoulders, enabling them to run very fast.

——————— S P O O R ———————

Similar in length to that of the sable antelope, but narrower. 7–9 cm long.

Actual size

Gemsbok
Oryx gazella

Afrikaans: Gemsbok
Ndebele: Nkukhama **Tswana:** Kukama
Herero: Ndumo **Nama/Damara:** ‖ Gaeb

DESCRIPTION

SHOULDER HEIGHT: 1,2 m **MASS:** 200 kg **GESTATION:** 240–270 days.
This gregarious, sure-footed and extremely swift antelope has very good eyesight. The horns are long and straight. A dangerous animal when wounded, the gembok has been known to impale lions on its pointed horns. It is fond of rolling. A nomadic animal, this species is often found in groups up to 40 strong. Old bulls lead solitary lives. The gemsbok is typically found on dry plains, in the desert and occasionally in savanna and mopane woodland.

DIET

Grazers. Will eat wild melons, cucumbers, bulbs and roots which are dug up using the forefeet. This species travels great distances for water, although it is largely independent of water as seen by the arid nature of the terrain it usually inhabits. Gemsbok are fond of mineral licks.

SPOOR

Heavy, splayed track; 11–13 cm long.

FAECES

One: slightly rounded, broad, flat end, tapered to a point. Up to 1,7 cm long.

11–13 cm

0   5 cm

Gemsbok have distinct, long, straight horns.

Red Hartebeest
Alcelaphus buselaphus

Afrikaans: Rooihartbees **Xhosa:** Xhama **Zulu:** Nduluzele
Tswana: Kgama **Sotho:** Thetele **Shona:** Ngama
Ndebele: Ndluzele **Nama/Damara:** | Khamab

DESCRIPTION

SHOULDER HEIGHT: 1,20–1,37 m MASS: 150–159 kg
GESTATION: 240 days; single young, born in summer.
Although fleet of foot, this species is preyed upon by lion, leopard and wild dogs. Both sexes have horns. It is a social animal found in large herds. A popular game-farming species, it is found over a wide area of South Africa; herds of up to 30 and more have also been found in the Kalahari.

DIET

Grazers, preferring medium-high grass which they feed on fairly selectively. Competition for good grazing areas is strong. Will drink regularly although capable of going for long periods without water. It is believed that these antelope derive moisture from shrubs, succulents and melons.

FAECES

Droppings are often found beneath *Acacia* trees, where they rest for long periods in the heat.

SPOOR

Almost identical to that of the tsessebe. 11–12 cm long.

0   5 cm

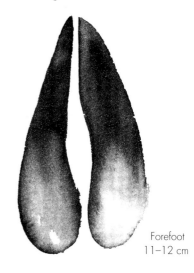

Forefoot
11–12 cm

The typical 'pronking' posture adopted by the red hartebeest when alarmed.

Sable
Hippotragus niger

Afrikaans: Swartwitpens **Zulu:** Mpalampale
Shangaan: Mhalamhala **Tswana:** Kwalata
Sotho, Venda: Phalafala **Ndebele:** Ngwaladi, Umtshwayeli
Shona: Mharapara, Ngwarati **Siswati:** Imphalampala
Lozi: Kwalata **Nama/Damara:** ǂNũ !nã | gaeb

DESCRIPTION

SHOULDER HEIGHT: 1,07–1,37 m **MASS:** 181–227 kg **GESTATION:** 270 days.
Bulls are often solitary or associate in small groups. Herds are usually led by a cow. Bulls are aggressive, fighting among themselves during association with cows. Hardy and tough, they will defend themselves against lion, leopard and dogs. When wounded they lie down and defend themselves with their razor-sharp horns. Both sexes have horns. When the females are ready to give birth, like the roan antelope, they leave the herd. The young remain hidden for the first month.

DIET

Ninety per cent of the diet consists of grass. Will feed on broad leaves to a certain extent. Dependent on water.

FAECES

1,5 cm long; well rounded with an indentation on one side.

0   5 cm

Both sexes carry horns but those of the cows are less robust.

SPOOR

Slightly shorter and narrower than that of the roan antelope and more pointed. 9 cm long.

Actual size

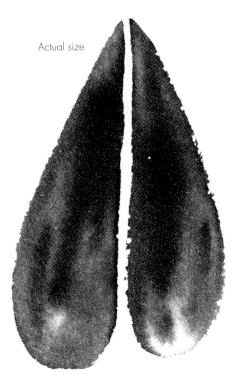

Roan Antelope
Hippotragus equinus

Afrikaans: Bastergemsbok   **Shona:** Ndunguza, Chengu
Ndebele: Ithaka   **Sotho:** Hlaba-ka-lela
Venda: Thavha-nda-lila   **Tswana:** Kunkuru, Kwalata, Esthetha
Shangaan: Ndakadsi   **Siswati:** Litagaezi   **Lozi:** Kwalata
Nama/Damara: !Hoa | nâ | gaeb

DESCRIPTION

SHOULDER HEIGHT: 1,3–1,5 m   **MASS:** 230–249 kg   **GESTATION:** 270 days.
The roan antelope is a compact, solidly built species. Small herds are led by a dominant cow. This is an aggressive species when fighting or wounded and utters a blowing snort when surprised. The ears are long with dark brown tassels at the tips. It has a well-developed mane with short, thick horns; both sexes have horns. The facial markings are conspicuous.

DIET

Predominantly a grazer; occasionally browses. Reliant on water. Susceptible to habitat change due to pressure from other species.

FAECES

Similar to that of the sable antelope.

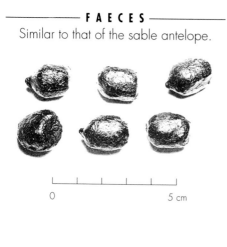

0   5 cm

A roan antelope bull.

Endangered species in South Africa

Roan antelope and tsessebe (rear) gathered at a waterhole.

Heart-shaped. When moving at speed, the hooves spread out. 10 cm long.

10 cm

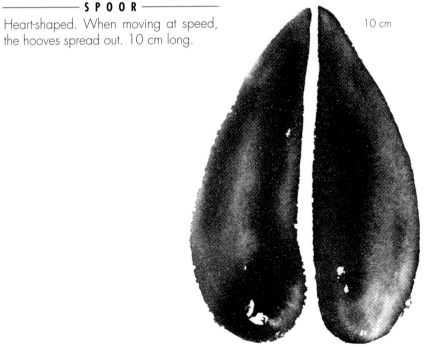

Puku
Kobus vardonii

Afrikaans: Poekoe
Lozi, Yei: Mutinya

DESCRIPTION

SHOULDER HEIGHT: 91–102 cm **MASS:** Up to 72 kg.

These antelope are found in the eastern Caprivi and in the Chobe National Park, Botswana. They occur in small herds, although males are often solitary. Puku also occur in Zambia, northwards to Tanzania. They prefer open grassland which borders swamps, vleis and rivers, and will always be found near water. The horns are shorter than the horns in the red lechwe and both males and females lack the black markings on the legs. This species feeds during the early morning and late evening, resting during the heat of the day.

DIET
Predominantly grazers.

FAECES
Round pellets. Collected in the Chobe National Park, Botswana.

0   5 cm

SPOOR
Broader and longer than that of the impala. 6–7 cm long.

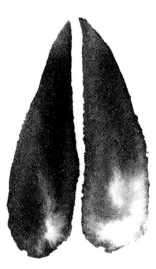

Actual size

Puku favour open grassland, bordering swamps, vleis and rivers.

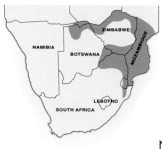

Waterbuck
Kobus ellipsiprymnus

Afrikaans: Waterbok   **Zulu, Siswati:** Phiva
Tswana: Pitlhwa   **Shangaan:** Mhitlwa   **Sotho:** Phitlwa
Ndebele: Isidumuka   **Venda:** Phidwa   **Shona:** Dhumukwa
Lozi: Ngunduma   **Nama/Damara:** ‖ Gampiris

DESCRIPTION

SHOULDER HEIGHT: 1,2 m   **MASS:** 200–250 kg   **GESTATION:** About 240 days.
This robust, well-built animal is found in small herds which are headed by a dominant bull. Bachelor herds are sometimes seen. It is preyed upon by lion and takes to water readily when pursued. It is found in stony or rocky areas, quite often some distance from water. Calves are commonly taken by leopard, cheetah and wild dogs. Waterbuck exude a heavy turpentine scent. The cow lacks horns.

DIET
Predominantly a grazer. They will however occasionally browse.

FAECES
The unusually large faeces are often found in a coagulated solid mass.

Loose form of pellets

Clustered pellets

The waterbuck has a distinctive white ring on its rear.

Distinctly heart-shaped. 7–9 cm long

Actual size

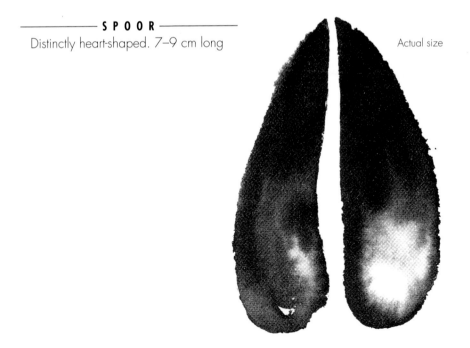

Red Lechwe
Kobus leche

Afrikaans: Basterwaterbok
Tswana: Letshwee
Lozi: Lizwii **Yei:** Unjya

DESCRIPTION

SHOULDER HEIGHT: 1 m **MASS:** Male 100 kg; female 77 kg
GESTATION: Between 215 and 248 days.

The red lechwe is found in the Caprivi, Namibia, and in the Okavango Delta of Botswana. It is a handsome, chestnut-coloured, highly gregarious animal. When alarmed, it bounds through the grass-covered *melapo* (lagoons) with strong splashes, horns laid back over the shoulders. It is not good at running on dry ground. It swims well, has excellent sight but a poor sense of smell. This species is preyed upon by lion, which ambush these antelope on the small islands and edges of the *melapo*, as well as by leopard, wild dog and cheetah. The red lechwe is also extensively hunted by the swamp-dwelling people who approach in a *mekoro* dugout, keeping well down below the grass height, until they are within shooting distance. Because of hunting pressure, this is a wary, shy animal.

DIET

A grazer; also feeds on aquatic plants. Feeds in water up to 60 cm deep. Prefers flood plains under shallow water.

FAECES

Compact, rounded pellets which are found on the edges of islands (formed when *melapos* dry out), lagoons and also in the water.

0   5 cm

When alarmed the red lechwe takes to water.

────── S P O O R ──────

Up to 8 cm long and pointed. The back of the pasterns are naked, as in the sitatunga. Spoor slightly splayed.

Actual size

Bushbuck
Tragelaphus scriptus

Afrikaans: Bosbok **Sotho:** Tshoso
Ndebele, Zulu, Swazi: Imbabala **Shona:** Dsoma
Xhosa: Imbabala **Shangaan:** Mbvala **Venda:** Mbavhala,
Tshishosho **Lozi:** Mbabala **Tswana:** Serolobotlhoko
Yei: Ungulungu **Nama/Damara:** !Garapiris

DESCRIPTION

SHOULDER HEIGHT: 69–94 cm **MASS:** 32–64 kg **GESTATION:** About 200 days.
An attractive, shy antelope inhabiting forest, riverine and dense bush. Widely distributed, it is territorial and usually found singly or in pairs. Although diurnal when undisturbed, it is primarily nocturnal and can be seen in the early morning and late evening. The senses are well developed; it is swift and jumps well. When wounded it becomes extremely aggressive. The voice is a loud, sharp bark. Bushbuck are preyed on by leopard, wild dogs in the Okavango Delta, and pythons lurking in the riverine vegetation.The Chobe bushbuck (*Tragelaphus scriptus ornatus*) is a subspecies found in the Chobe National Park, Botswana. It is more distinctly marked and has a long bushy tail. Bushbuck are often found in the company of baboons.

DIET
Seed pods, twigs, shoots, leaves, wild fruits and roots.

FAECES
Single pellets, often clustered together.

0   5 cm

The bushbuck varies from light to dark brown in colour according to the region.

───── SPOOR ─────

Neater and smaller than the impala.
4–5 cm long.

Actual size

Nyala
Tragelaphus angasii

Afrikaans: Njala
Shona: Nyara **Siswati:** Litagayezi
Ndebele, Zulu, Shangaan, Venda: Inyala

DESCRIPTION

SHOULDER HEIGHT: 91–107 cm **MASS:** 100–126 kg **GESTATION:** 252 days.

This is a handsome, striking antelope which inhabits dense bush and riverine vegetation offering cover. It has a deep bark similar to that of a bushbuck. It is common in the reserves of KwaZulu-Natal, the northern Kruger National Park, southeastern Zimbabwe and Mozambique. The male is conspicuously different from the female in colour and size; it has a shaggy coat (well-developed on the underbelly), a bushy tail, large ears, and a distinctive white chevron between the eyes. The sides are marked with numerous white stripes. The female is lighter in colour than the male and lacks horns. Nyala congregate in herds of up to 30 strong, although solitary animals are not uncommon. It moves freely by day.

DIET

Primarily a browser, but will also graze.

FAECES

Round to spherical pellets, can be up to 1,5 cm long.

SPOOR

Similar shape to that of the bushbuck, but somewhat longer. 5–6 cm long.

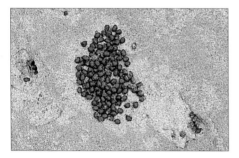

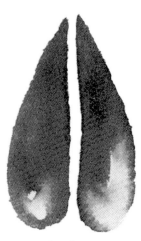

Actual size

Female and calf at the water's edge.   Insert: Male drinking.

195

Sitatunga
Tragelaphus spekei

Afrikaans: Waterkoedoe
Tswana: Nakong
Lozi: Situtunga **Yei:** Unzunzu

DESCRIPTION

SHOULDER HEIGHT: 1,0 –1,14 m **MASS:** 70–110 kg **GESTATION:** Little is known.
This shy, retiring animal is found in the Okavango Delta, Botswana, and in the Caprivi, Namibia. It is larger than bushbuck with a bark similar to that of the other *Tragelaphus* species: kudu, nyala and bushbuck. When disturbed, it immerses itself in water leaving only the nose visible. A good swimmer, this diurnal species spends the greater part of the day immersed in water. They are preyed upon by lion which move from island to island, and when they venture into woodland, also by wild dogs and leopard. It generally moves at a slow pace and thus avoids detection.

DIET
A browser and grazer, it eats aquatic vegetation.

FAECES
Similar to that of the impala. Difficult to find due to sitatunga's retiring nature and habit of spending long periods immersed in water.

0   5 cm

The sitatunga feeds on reeds and grass.

SPOOR

A distinctive elongated hoof which splays out, enabling it to move over marsh and swamp vegetation.

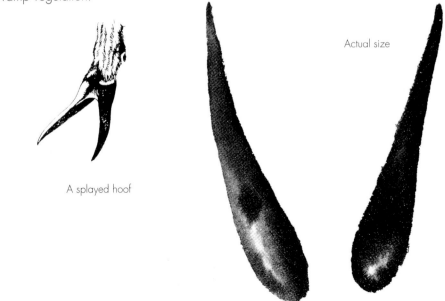

Actual size

A splayed hoof

Kudu
Tragelaphus strepsiceros

Afrikaans: Koedoe **Zulu:** Mgankla
Xhosa: Qudu **Shangaan:** Hlongo
Siswati: Shongololo **Sotho, Venda, Tswana:** Tholo
Shona: Nhoro **Ndebele:** Ibhalabhala **Lozi:** Tolo
Yei: Unzwa **Nama/Damara:** Xaib

DESCRIPTION

SHOULDER HEIGHT: 1,2 m **MASS:** 150–270 kg **GESTATION:** About 210 days.
These gregarious animals are found in herds of up to 12. Bulls are either solitary or in groups – 14 mature bulls have been observed in one group in the Tuli Block, Botswana. Kudu are found in well-bushed regions and in hills. Shy, timid animals, they are most adept at concealment, remaining motionless for long periods when suspicious. They approach water carefully and are largely mobile at night. Their call is a loud bark and their sight, sense of smell and hearing are all excellent.

DIET

Browsers; fruit, seed pods, melons and young grass shoots. Also raid crops. Fairly independent of water.

FAECES

Compact, rounded pellets similar to those of a young giraffe.

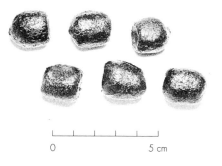

0   5 cm

The kudu bull has long, distinctive, spiral horns.

SPOOR

Longer and more pointed than that of the nyala; similar in length to the blue wildebeest, if it is a large bull, but not as splayed. 8–9 cm long.

Actual size

Eland
Taurotragus oryx

Afrikaans: Eland **Zulu, Xhosa:** Mpofu
Shangaan: Mhofu **Sotho:** Phohu, Phofu
Venda, Tswana: Phofu **Shona:** Mhofu
Ndebele: Impofu **Siswati:** Impophi **Lozi:** Pofu
Yei: Unshefu **Nama/Damara:** !Khanni

─────────── **D E S C R I P T I O N** ───────────

SHOULDER HEIGHT: 1,5–1,75 m **MASS:** Up to 900 kg
GESTATION: Between 255 and 265 days; single calf.

These inoffensive, gregarious, but shy, animals are excellent jumpers. They are nomadic, inhabiting savannas and open plains, dry mopane, light woodland and montane grassland. Independent of water, eland derive their moisture intake from plants. Both sexes have horns; although those of the females are often longer Old bulls are often solitary. Normally silent creatures, eland have an acute sense of smell, and good hearing.

─────────── **D I E T** ───────────

Mainly browsers, but will also graze. Fond of young grass in areas that have been burnt. Eat leaves, wild fruits, bulbs and the bark of certain trees, particularly wortel-doring, *Sesamothamnus lugardii*. The horns play a useful role in rendering branches accessible. Obtains moisture from its food sources.

─────────── **F A E C E S** ───────────

Large, well rounded pellets.

0   5 cm

The largest of all the African antelope.

Largest spoor of all the antelopes;
11–14 cm long. Well splayed.

11–14 cm long

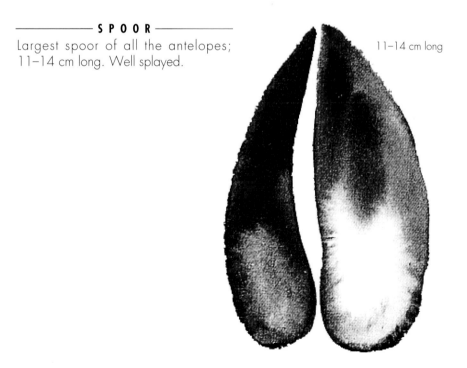

Buffalo
Syncerus caffer

DESCRIPTION

SHOULDER HEIGHT: 1,5 m **MASS:** 600 kg **GESTATION:** 330 days; single calf; breeds throughout the year with peaks in August and September.

These are gregarious, shy creatures with fair sight, poor to good hearing and a good sense of smell. When pursued and wounded they are particularly dangerous. If you approach them on foot, they will stare in your direction before finally running off uttering grunts. It is wise to avoid dense cover and reeds where old bulls may be lying up. They charge head-on and are difficult to stop at short range. Good swimmers, they are fond of wallowing. The boss (heavy part of the horn which rests on the animal's head) and horns are used to smash bushes. They are preyed upon by lion which are invariably found trailing large herds.

DIET

Grazer, but occasionally browses on shoots, twigs and bushes. Dependent on water; therefore limited in distribution by availability of water.

FAECES

Unmistakably cow-like; often loose. Dark in colour, turning whitish brown with age. Freshness is tested by breaking open the surface of the dropping.

Buffalo prefer open woodland savanna with an abundance of suitable grass.

SPOOR

Large and circular in shape. Almost identical to domestic cattle. Gait slow and ponderous.

The circular forefoot

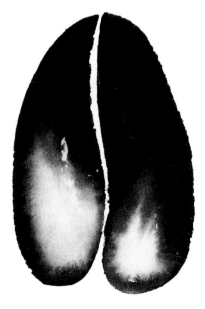

Hind foot
12–15 cm

Comparative Spoor Illustrations

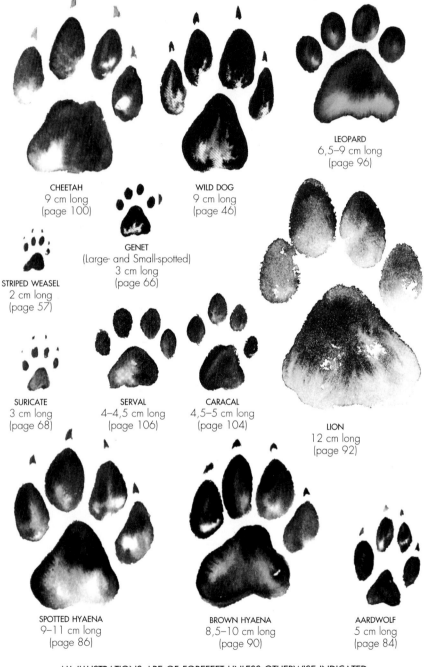

LEOPARD
6,5–9 cm long
(page 96)

CHEETAH
9 cm long
(page 100)

WILD DOG
9 cm long
(page 46)

GENET
(Large- and Small-spotted)
3 cm long
(page 66)

STRIPED WEASEL
2 cm long
(page 57)

SURICATE
3 cm long
(page 68)

SERVAL
4–4,5 cm long
(page 106)

CARACAL
4,5–5 cm long
(page 104)

LION
12 cm long
(page 92)

SPOTTED HYAENA
9–11 cm long
(page 86)

BROWN HYAENA
8,5–10 cm long
(page 90)

AARDWOLF
5 cm long
(page 84)

ALL ILLUSTRATIONS ARE OF FOREFEET UNLESS OTHERWISE INDICATED.

| AFRICAN WILD CAT 3,4 cm long (page 108) | SMALL SPOTTED CAT 2,1 cm long (page 110) | DWARF MONGOOSE 2 cm long (page 82) | MELLER'S MONGOOSE 2,9 cm long (page 70) | SLENDER MONGOOSE 2,5 cm long (page 79) |

| SELOUS' MONGOOSE 3–5 cm long (page 71) | WATER MONGOOSE 4 cm long (page 76) | WHITE-TAILED MONGOOSE 4 cm long (page 75) | LARGE GREY MONGOOSE 4 cm long (page 78) | BANDED MONGOOSE 3,5 cm long (page 80) |

STRIPED POLECAT 2,5 cm long (page 56)

| CAPE FOX 5 cm long (page 48) | BAT-EARED FOX 3,5–4 cm long (page 50) | | AFRICAN CIVET 5 cm long (page 64) | SPOTTED-NECKED OTTER 4–4,5 cm long (page 60) |

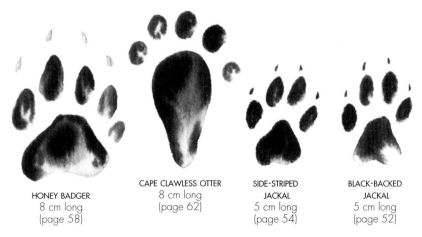

| | HONEY BADGER 8 cm long (page 58) | CAPE CLAWLESS OTTER 8 cm long (page 62) | SIDE-STRIPED JACKAL 5 cm long (page 54) | BLACK-BACKED JACKAL 5 cm long (page 52) |

ALL ILLUSTRATIONS ARE OF FOREFEET UNLESS OTHERWISE INDICATED.

SUNI	**GRYSBOK**	**SHARPE'S GRYSBOK**	**RED DUIKER**	**BLUE DUIKER**	**COMMON DUIKER**
2,5 cm long	2,5 cm long	2,5 cm long	2,4 cm long	2 cm long	3 cm long
(page 148)	(page 150)	(page 151)	(page 155)	(page 154)	(page 156)

ORIBI
3 cm long
(page 146)

KLIPSPRINGER
3 cm long
(page 153)

BLESBOK
6 cm long
(page 160)

DAMARA DIK-DIK
2 cm long
(page 144)

STEENBOK
2,6 cm long
(page 158)

REEDBUCK
6 cm long
(page 164)

BONTEBOK
7 cm long
(page 162)

MOUNTAIN REEDBUCK
4,5–5 cm long
(page 166)

GEMSBOK
11–13 cm long
(page 178)

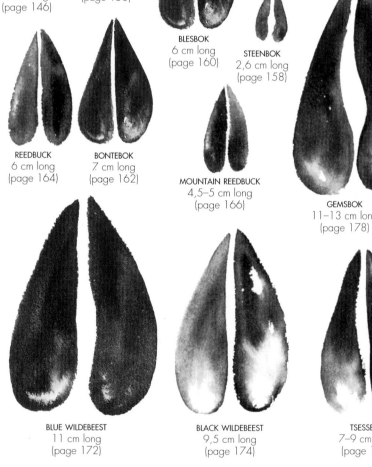

BLUE WILDEBEEST
11 cm long
(page 172)

BLACK WILDEBEEST
9,5 cm long
(page 174)

TSESSEBE
7–9 cm long
(page 176)

ALL ILLUSTRATIONS ARE OF FOREFEET UNLESS OTHERWISE INDICATED.

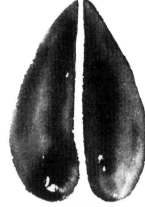

SABLE
9 cm long
(page 182)

ROAN ANTELOPE
10–11 cm long
(page 184)

RED HARTEBEEST
11–12 cm long
(page 180)

KUDU
8–9 cm long
(page 198)

PUKU
6–7 cm long
(page 186)

SPRINGBOK
5 cm long
(page 168)

NYALA
5–6 cm long
(page 194)

BUSHBUCK
4–6 cm long
(page 192)

IMPALA
4–6 cm long
(page 170)

WATERBUCK
9 cm long
(page 188)

RED LECHWE
7–8 cm long
(page 190)

SITATUNGA
7 cm long
(page 196)

ALL ILLUSTRATIONS ARE OF FOREFEET UNLESS OTHERWISE INDICATED.

WARTHOG
5 cm long
(page 138)

BUSHPIG
6 cm long
(page 136)

Fore

Hind

PANGOLIN
4–5 cm long
(page 32)

AARDVARK
7–7,5 cm long
(page 112)

ELAND
11–14 cm long
(page 200)

MOUNTAIN ZEBRA
10 cm long
(page 134)

BURCHELL'S ZEBRA
10–11 cm long
(page 132)

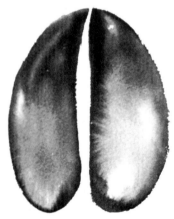

BUFFALO
12–15 cm long
(page 202)

GIRAFFE
19 cm long
(page 142)

ALL ILLUSTRATIONS ARE OF FOREFEET UNLESS OTHERWISE INDICATED.

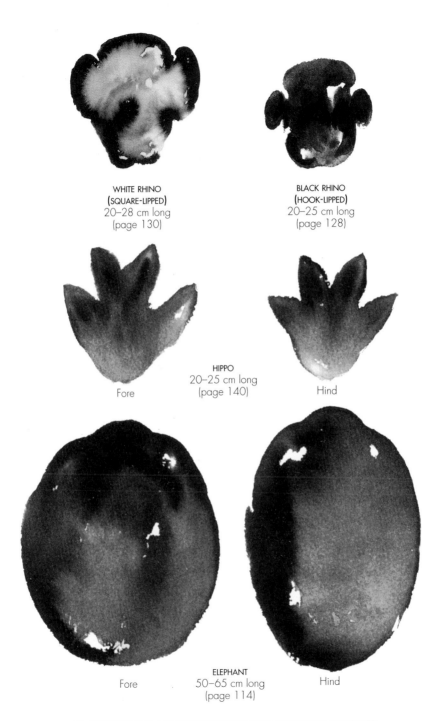

**WHITE RHINO
(SQUARE-LIPPED)**
20–28 cm long
(page 130)

**BLACK RHINO
(HOOK-LIPPED)**
20–25 cm long
(page 128)

HIPPO
20–25 cm long
(page 140)

Fore

Hind

ELEPHANT
50–65 cm long
(page 114)

Fore

Hind

ALL ILLUSTRATIONS ARE OF FOREFEET UNLESS OTHERWISE INDICATED.

LESSER BUSHBABY
3 cm long
(page 22)

THICK-TAILED BUSHBABY
3,5 cm long
(page 24)

Hind

VERVET MONKEY
5,5 cm long
(page 26)

SAMANGO MONKEY
6,6 cm long
(page 28)

CHACMA BABOON
15–16 cm long
(page 30)

Hind

Fore
Hind

SCRUB HARE
3,2 cm long
(page 34)

Fore
Hind

TREE SQUIRREL
2,3 cm long
(page 40)

HEDGEHOG
1,5–2 cm long
(page 20)

Fore
Hind

SPRINGHARE
3,2 cm long
(page 42)

Fore
Hind

**ROCK AND YELLOW-
SPOTTED DASSIES**
4,2 cm long
(pages 122,124)

Fore

PORCUPINE
9,5 cm long
(page 44)

Hind

ALL ILLUSTRATIONS ARE OF FOREFEET UNLESS OTHERWISE INDICATED.

Bibliography

Astley Maberley. 1967, *The Game Animals of Southern Africa,*
Don Nelson Publishers, Cape Town.
Dorst, J. and Dandelot, P. 1970, *A Field Guide to the Larger Mammals of Africa,*
Collins, London.
Estes, R.D. 1993, *The Safari Companion,* Russel Friedman Books, Johannesburg.
Grobelaar, H., Hall-Martin, A., Walker, C. 1984, *Predators of Southern Africa,*
Southern Book Publishers, Johannesburg.
Kenmuir, D. and Williams, R. 1975, *Wild Mammals,* Bundu Series,
Longman, Rhodesia.
Liebenberg, L. 1992, *A Concise Guide to the Animal Tracks of Southern Africa,*
David Phillip Publishers, Cape Town and Johannesburg.
Lyell, D. 1929, *The Hunting and Spoor of Central African Game,*
Seeley, Service and Co. Limited, London.
Merz, A. 1991, *Rhino at the brink of extinction,*
Harper Collins Publishers, South Africa.
Smithers, R.H.N. 1966, *The Mammals of Rhodesia, Zambia and Malawi,*
Collins, London.
Smithers, R.H.N. 1984, *The Mammals of the Southern African Subregion,*
University of Pretoria, Pretoria.
Smithers, R.H.N. 1986, *Land Mammals of Southern Africa,*
MacMillan Publishers, South Africa.
Stuart, C. and T. 1988, *Field Guide to the Mammals of Southern Africa,*
Struik Publishers, Cape Town.
Swanepoel, P., Smithers, R.H.N. and Rautenbach, I.L. 1980,
A Checklist and numbering system of the extant Mammals of the Southern African subregion,
Annals of the Transvaal Museum, 32(7):156–196.
Zaloumis, E.A. and Cross, R. 1974, *Antelope of Southern Africa,*
Wildlife Society.

Blue wildebeest spoor

White (square-lipped) rhinoceros

Photographic Credits

Clive Walker: pp 2, 6, 8, 9, 10, 11, 17 (bottom left and top right), 18 (left), 19, 21 (bottom), 39, 47, 59, 62, 77, 81, 86, 89, 90, 93, 94, 95, 98 (left), 105, 115, 117, 118, 121, 130 (right), 131, 140, 138, 184, 203, 212, back cover, all spoor and faeces;
Alan Weaving: pp 21(top), 37, 67 (top), 107, 145, 189;
Lex Hes: pp 25, 197;
Nigel Dennis/SIL: pp 27, 101, 109, 133, 135, 141, 155, 181, back cover (bottom);
Nigel Dennis: pp 16, 17 (top left), 31 (top), 65, 83 (bottom), 99 (bottom), 103, 129, 177, 199, spine (top), front cover (bottom left);
Rob Haestier: p 29;
Peter Pickford/SIL: pp 33, 35, 97, 98 (right), 99 (top), 169, 171, front cover (middle);
Daryl Balfour: pp 41, 49, 85, 87, 183, 185, 187;
Peter Lillie: p 51;
Roger de la Harpe/SIL: p 53;
C&T Stuart: pp 57, 61;
Hein von Hörsten/ABPL: p 67 (bottom);
T.P Jackson: p 69;
Phillip van den Berg/HPH Photography: pp 73, 175;
P.I. Chadwick: pp 91, 139;
Lanz von Hörsten: pp 125, 173;
Anthony Bannister: pp 56, 137;
Andrew Bannister/SIL: p 83 (top);
Mike Bruorton: p 143;
S H M David: p 150;
JC Paterson-Jones: pp 157, 159, 179, 195 (insert);
Vic Peddemors: p 161;
Anthony H. Martin: p 14;
Anthony H. Martin/© Clive Walker: pp 15, 18 (right), 55, 153, 163;
Colin Bell/© Clive Walker: front cover (right);
Les Hex/Photo Access: pp 23, 75;
Brendan Ryan/ABPL: p 42; ABPL: p 43;
J&B Photographers/Photo Access: pp 45, 193;
HPH Photographers/Photo Access: pp 63, 147, 149, 151, 152, 154, 165, 167, 201;
Peter Steyn/Photo Access: pp 74, 127;
AJ Stevens/ABPL: p 111;
Keith Bess/ABPL: p 113;
David Steele/Photo Access: p 123;
Koos Bothma: p 145 (bottom);
CF Bartlett/Photo Access: p 185;
Gerald Cubitt: back cover, front cover (bottom middle);
Roger de la Harpe: pp 191, 195 (main), front cover (top).

Index to Common Names

Aardvark 112
Aardwolf 84
Antelope, Roan 184
Baboon, Chacma 30
Blesbok 160
Bontebok 162
Buffalo 202
Bushbaby, Lesser 22
  Thick-tailed 24
Bushbuck 192
Caracal 104
Cat, African Wild 108
  Small Spotted 110
Cheetah 100
Civet, African 64
Dassie, Rock 124
  Tree 122
  Yellow-spotted Rock 126
Dik-dik, Damara 144
Dog, Wild 46
Duiker, Blue 154
  Common 156
  Red 155
Eland 200
Elephant 114
Fox, Bat-eared 50
  Cape 48
Gemsbok 178
Genets,
  Large-spotted 66
  Small-spotted 66
Giraffe 142

Grysbok 150
  Sharpe's 151
Hare, Cape 36
  Scrub 34
  Spring 42
Hartebeest, Red 180
Hedgehog 20
Hippopotamus 140
Honey Badger 58
Hyaena, Brown 90
  Spotted 86
Impala 170
Jackal, Black-backed 52
  Side-striped 54
Klipspringer 153
Kudu 198
Lechwe, Red 190
Leopard 96
Lion 92
Mongoose,
  Banded 80
  Small Grey 74
  Dwarf 82
  Large Grey 78
  Meller's 70
  Selous' 71
  Slender 79
  Water 76
  White-tailed 75
  Yellow 72
Monkey, Samango 28
Vervet 26

Nyala 194
Oribi 146
Otter, Cape Clawless 62
  Spotted-necked 60
Pangolin 32
Pig, Bush- 136
Polecat, Striped 56
Porcupine 44
Puku 186
Rat, Greater Cane 43
Reedbuck 164
Reedbuck, Mountain 166
Rhebuck, Grey 152
Rhinoceros, Black 128
Rhinoceros, White 130
Sable 182
Serval 106
Sitatunga 196
Springbok 168
Squirrel, Ground 38
  Tree 40
Steenbok 158
Suni 148
Suricate 68
Tsessebe 176
Warthog 138
Waterbuck 188
Weasel, Striped 57
Wildebeest, Black 174
  Blue 172
Zebra, Burchell's 132
  Mountain 135

Index to Scientific Names

Acinonyx jubatus	100	Genetta genetta	66	Panthera leo	92
Aepyceros melampus	170	Genetta tigrina	66	Panthera pardus	96
Alcelaphus buselaphus	180	Giraffa camelopardalis	142	Papio ursinus	30
Antidorcas marsupialis	168	Helogale parvula	82	Paracynictis selousi	71
Aonyx capensis	62	Herpestes ichneumon	78	Paraxerus cepapi	40
Atelerix frontalis	20	Heterohyrax brucei	126	Pedetes capensis	42
Atilax paludinosus	76	Hippopotamus amphibius	140	Pelea capreolus	152
Canis adustus	54	Hippotragus equinus	184	Phacochoerus aethiopicus	138
Canis mesomelas	52	Hippotragus niger	182	Poecilogale albinucha	57
Cephalophus natalensis	155	Hyaena brunnea	90	Potamochoerus porcus	136
Ceratotherium simum	130	Hystrix africaeaustralis	44	Procavia capensis	124
Cercopithecus aethiops	26	Ichneumia albicauda	75	Proteles cristatus	84
Cercopithecus mitis	28	Ictonyx striatus	56	Raphicerus campestris	158
Civettictus civetta	64	Kobus ellipsiprymnus	188	Raphicerus sharpei	151
Connochaetes gnou	174	Kobus leche	190	Raphicerus melanotis	150
Connochaetes taurinus	172	Kobus vardonii	186	Redunca arundinum	164
Crocuta crocuta	86	Lepus capensis	36	Redunca fulvorufula	166
Cynictis penicillata	72	Lepus saxatilis	34	Rhynchogale melleri	70
Damaliscus dorcas dorcas	162	Loxodonta africana	114	Suricata suricatta	68
Damaliscus dorcas phillipsi	160	Lutra maculicollis	60	Sylvicapra grimmia	156
Damaliscus lunatus	176	Lycaon pictus	46	Syncerus caffer	202
Dendrohyrax arboreus	122	Madoqua kirkii	144	Taurotragus oryx	200
Diceros bicornis	128	Manis temminckii	32	Thryonomys swinderianus	43
Equus burchellii	132	Mellivora capensis	58	Tragelaphus angasii	194
Equus zebra zebra	134	Mungos mungo	80	Tragelaphus scriptus	192
Felis caracal	104	Neotragus moschatus	148	Tragelaphus spekei	196
Felis lybica	108	Oreotragus oreotragus	153	Tragelaphus strepsiceros	198
Felis nigripes	110	Orycteropus afer	112	Vulpes chama	48
Felis serval	106	Oryx gazella	178	Xerus inauris	38
Galago moholi	22	Otocyon megalotis	50		
Galerella pulverulenta	74	Otolemur crassicaudatus	24		
Galerella sanguinea	79	Ourebia ourebi	146		